U.S.L.H.S.

1789 - 1939

# Lighthouses of Southern New England

## A Pictorial Guide

*Brant Point Light   Nantucket, Massachusetts*

# Lighthouses of Southern New England

## A Pictorial Guide

Courtney Thompson

Designed, edited and published by
CatNap Publications


ISBN: 0-9714178-0-6
Library of Congress Catalog Card Number: 2001-129329

Photography and editing: Courtney Thompson

Maps and graphics:
Courtney Thompson
Rusty Nelson, South Portland, ME.

Narrative material:
Jeremy D'Entremont, Portsmouth, NH.
Ted Panayotoff, Camden, ME.

Original artwork:
Artwork by *Maloue* (M. Louise Young Shaw), Page 112


Printed in Canada by Quebecor Atlantic
St. John, New Brunswick    Canada

For purchase information please contact:
CatNap Publications    (800)  720-4751

*For my mother. Her support and love made this project possible*

# Table of Contents

# Lighthouses of Massachusetts

## Cape Ann & North Shore

## Salem Shore

## Boston Harbor

## South Shore

# Lighthouses of Massachusetts

## Southeastern Shore

## Cape Cod

## Martha's Vineyard & Nantucket

# Lighthouses of Rhode Island

# Lighthouses of Connecticut

# Lighthouses of Connecticut

# Introduction

The maritime history of Massachusetts, Rhode Island and Connecticut is a vivid one, replete with images and tales of shipwrecks, heroism, pirates and pilgrims. Whaling, fishing and international shipping also were important elements of that history and lighthouses an integral part of the story. The sea and safe passage upon the water were essential to life and times when transportation was primarily by boat and settlement concentrated near and along the coast. Lighthouses offer a tangible reminder of a time when life was of a simpler vein yet in many ways presented more rigorous challenges. During the 18th and 19th centuries lighthouses were the mariners' guide to the waterways, but were always themselves to some degree at the mercy of the sea's power.

Primarily, lighthouses represented safety and certainty to early mariners, reassurance and constant point of reference amid changing seas, unpredictable weather and dangerous journeys. They evoke today a similar sense and strength of purpose. The lights are at once peaceful, lonely, beautiful, forlorn, silent or raucous, signaling both welcome and warning-- subject often to harsh, unforgiving conditions yet in locations of breathtaking beauty. A benevolent appearance under clear skies and calm seas often becomes an aura of foreboding and loneliness brought about by dense fog or a powerful 'noreaster. Lighthouses which host summer visitors, in winter become wonderfully deserted and peaceful; those which in summer offer a challenging, appealing destination for vacationing sailors become isolated and face winter's storms head on.

With advances in navigational tools and techniques it's noted that the technical function of the lighthouse is no longer the vital element it once was. The intangible elements which these structures provide, however, are significant and irreplaceable. This book is intended to offer a comprehensive pictorial tour of the lighthouses of the three southern New England states. The historic images are included to provide a glimpse into the past, when lighthouses all were vital, functioning and peopled; dates are noted when possible. Maps and directions give specific routes to and/or sense of location for each beacon. The collection of multiple photographs, historic images, maps, directions and narrative notes into one volume offers a complete look at each lighthouse, hopefully comparable to a "walk" or trip around the grounds.

Completion of this project involved travel over well-known routes, discovery of little-used back roads, and exploration of coves and islands. Many people were gracious in their assistance and I was privileged to gain access to private properties and special locations. Everyone I met during this adventure was helpful, cooperative and encouraging. In particular, the Massachusetts narratives were compiled from the generous contribution of material by Jeremy D'Entrement gathered for his projects, representing hours of research, compilation and writing. Additionally, Ted Panayotoff researched and compiled material for the Connecticut and Rhode Island historical overviews; both Ted and Jo Panayotoff have been valuable consultants throughout the project.

Finally, my thanks to all others who helped me along the way.

# The Lighthouse Tradition

## Early History: Looking Back

Throughout most of recorded history lighthouses have not only aided mariners in navigation but also represented unique architectural reflections of cultural development. As man began to cross the seas and oceans to trade civilization spread; navigational aids were a mark of expanding explorations and technology. Lighthouses have evolved from fires burning on hilltops to modern masonry or steel-frame structures capable of resisting the severest storms.

Although the Phoenicians and Egyptians are thought to have built lighthouses, no records document their construction; priests likely were the first "lightkeepers", building bonfires at landfalls in Egypt. Completed in Alexandria, Egypt in the third century B.C., the Pharos of Alexandria is the first lighthouse which is documented with detailed accounts. The stone structure with wood fire on top was built c. 280 BC at the mouth of Alexandria Harbor and thought to be the world's first lighthouse. Thereafter, "pharos" came to mean "lighthouse"; the science of lighthouse construction and illumination became "pharology". Considered one of the Seven Wonders of the World, with elaborate carvings and ornamentation, for more than 1500 years the structure functioned as an aid to navigation, withstanding damage sustained by invaders and earthquakes, until it finally succumbed in the 14th century. As the Roman Empire spread across Europe, lighthouses followed; existence of more than 30 lighthouses throughout the widespread Roman provinces has been documented. Most coastal lights did not survive the Dark Ages although some monastic orders kept fires burning near their coastal monasteries. In some English parishes lights were placed in church towers, giving rise to the tradition that lighting the coasts was the work of Christian charity.

Trading among European nations increased at the end of the Dark Ages (about 1100), resulting in increased shipping activity and construction of more lighthouses particularly in England, France, Germany and Italy. The formalization of lighthouse service was a result of the suppression of monastic orders during the reign of Henry VIII. In 1565 the first statute dealing with lighthouses in Great Britain was enacted, creating the Corporation of the Trinity House. The law noted that the Corporation *"shall....erect and set up...beacons, marks and signs for the sea, in such place or places.....whereby dangers may be avoided and escaped and ships the better come into their ports without peril."* Although a boon to mariners, the navigational aids were not welcomed by all coastal dwellers; those who depended on shipwrecks as a source of fuel and goods vocally opposed the construction of beacons. Nevertheless, the number of major lighthouses increased dramatically during the age of discovery and colonial trade in the 16th and 17th centuries.

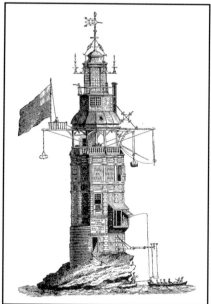

*Early Eddystone tower*

## Construction

The golden age of tower design was seen in the early centuries of lighthouse construction. Most Old World towers were of stone masonry construction, located at important ports. As rapid advances in equipment and construction occured in the 1700s, the first towers completely exposed to the sea were built-- notably the Eddystone Light fourteen miles offshore from the port of Plymouth, England. The successive forms of this structure mirrored increasingly scientific design principles.

In 1696-1699 a massive wooden tower was built on the rock, anchored by twelve iron stanchions. Destroyed by storm in 1703, the tower was rebuilt in 1708 in the form of a slender, tapering wooden structure built around a central timber mast. When this tower burned in 1755, it was replaced with masonry blocks dovetailed together to form a curved profile to resist wind and waves, a design which soon became standard. In 1882 the present lighthouse was built, nearly twice the height of the previous, resting on a solid masonry base, with foundation stones dovetailed into each other and into the reef. Lighthouses at other isolated spots were then patterned after Eddystone.

The 16th and 17th centuries saw rapid expansion of trade from Europe to the Americas, with construction of lighthouses in North America following the pattern seen in Europe. In both Canadian and American colonies, the first lights were located at important harbors-- the first in the United States in Boston Harbor, the first in Canada at Louisburg, Cape Breton. Both initial structures were destroyed by the British armies. Lighthouses and keeper's quarters in colonial America were primarily built of stone, with functionality and simplicity uppermost in design objectives. With a few exceptions, most lighthouses in the Atlantic colonies in Canada were built of wood. Availability of the resource and low cost enabled timely construction of wood structures. Given the harsh and damp marine climate, these structures proved surprisingly durable; the lighthouse at Gannet Rock in the Bay of Fundy has withstood the elements since construction in 1831.

## Fuel & Illumination Systems

Most early lights were harbor lights, often so feeble that a vigorous debate arose whether lights should be used to warn mariners to steer clear of dangers or to guide them to a safe location. The argument was not without merit. In these early beacons, the source of light was typically an open fire atop the tower, subject to the elements. Fires were fueled by wood taken from the area, often eliminating the nearby forest in short order. Open fires, using wood or candles, were not generally reliable, often sputtering out or causing fires. Additionally, a strong wind determined the effectiveness of the light; blustery winds from the land produced brighter light to seaward, thus aiding mariners, whereas stiff sea breezes were likely to diminish the flame seen by mariners at sea. Rain also was a key factor, making presence of the flame erratic in storms; not until later years were lanterns enclosed, often with glazed material which also reduced the visibility of the light if not kept meticulously clean.

*Open coal fire*

Coal became standard after 1500 because it burned more slowly than wood and produced a better light. Wind was again a significant factor however. When buffetted by strong winds, coal fires often generated sufficient heat to melt or damage the grate container. During fog or rain it was however possible that the glow from the open fires might be reflected in the atmosphere much like the linger of the sun's glow at sunset. It wasn't until the middle of the 19th century that open coal fires were discontinued, the last extinguished in England in 1823.

Swiss-born Aime Argand is credited with a major technological advancement in illumination. The Argand lamp--an oil lamp with circular wick protected by glass chimney-- was invented in 1782 and was the principle lighthouse illuminant for more than a century. The lamp was combined with reflectors to produce a bright, concentrated light which was not diffused and thereby lost. Sperm oil was typically used as fuel, although others were tried with varying degrees of success, including seal, porpoise, and cod liver oil. Animal-based oils were later replaced by vegetable oils, such as colza, refined from rapeseed. A Canadian, Abraham Gesner, in 1846 made a further significant contribution to lighting technology with the invention of coal oil, or kerosene. Used in flat-wick lamps, kerosene was the standard illuminant until the turn of the century and the advent of petroleum and acetylene lamps. In the late 18th and early 19th century the incandescent oil vapor lamp came into use, creating a bright light well suited to the Fresnel lens.

Light beams are captured and concentrated by two means: the rays can be reflected with mirrors (catoptric principle) or they can be deflected by passing them through lenses (dioptric principle). Reflectors and refractors were designed to focus, or concentrate, the light into a single powerful beam. The catoptric reflector (1777) consisted of hundreds of mirror sections set in a plaster mold in the form of a parabolic curve. Silvered copper reflectors later replaced these. The resulting beam of light then had to be rotated by clockwork mechanism in order to be visible from any direction. Bowl-shaped mirrors of varying diameter were grouped behind the light to increase the power of an Argand lamp up to seven-fold. This apparatus could become cumbersome and often almost entirely filled the lantern room.

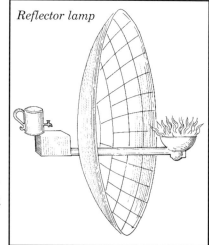

*Reflector lamp*

The next, and key, breakthrough in lighthouse optics was the introduction of lenses, specifically those designed by Augustin Fresnel. Fresnel was an engineer and pioneer in the study of optics. He began his research in 1814 and by 1822 had perfected the dioptric system, a lighthouse lens superior to anything previously developed. Glass prisms at the center of a bull's eye lens magnified the light, sending out a thin, horizontal beam of concentrated light. Fresnel later added reflecting prisms above and below, producing the catadioptric system, the basis of optical systems in lighthouses today. Illumination was originally from a lamp inside the lens; lamps for smaller lenses required one or two circular wicks with four or five required for larger lenses placed one inside the other.

The order or size of the Fresnel lens was determined by the distance of the flame from the lens, or focal distance. Numbered one through six, the first order lens had the greatest focal length, the sixth order the shortest. Similarly, the first order lens had the largest diameter and sixth the smallest. Used primarily in seacoast lights, the first-order Fresnel lens weighed up to six tons; the small fourth and fifth order lenses weighed 200-300 pounds. A fixed light was produced by a lens with smooth glass at its center belt; a glass molded into the form of a bull's eye at the center belt was used for a flashing light with rotation of the lens via clockwork mechanism producing the flashing effect. In 1890 a method was devised to rotate the lights by floating the apparatus on a bed of mercury, thereby virtually eliminating friction and permitting revolutions as frequently as every 15 seconds.

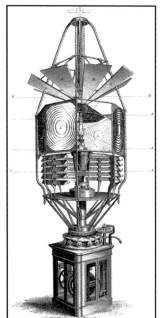

*Early Fresnel rotating mechanism*

## Identification

Improvements in lighting technology made the lights more visible and four international light classifications were defined according to size and intenstiy: landfall, major coastal, secondary coastal and harbor. However, for the mariner the problem of distinguishing between lighthouses, especially those relatively close together, was a significant one. Mistaking one light for another was often a fatal error. For identification in daylight hours, the structures were painted with disinctive "daymarks", typically colored stripes or bands, which made the lighthouse stand out from the land. White was found to show up best against land, even in snow; red or black stripes, bands or lantern rooms further distinguished a specific structure.

Accurate identification of the lights at night presented yet another challenge. Rotation of the light was the first intervention; placement of reflectors or screens caused the rotating light to flash or occult. A flashing light displays the beam for a shorter time than the subsequent period of darkness; the reverse pattern produces an occulting light. Rotation of the light was initially accomplished by a weight-driven clockwork mechanism, similar to that used in grandfather clocks. The keeper was required to wind the mechansim every few hours. The advent of the electric motor eliminated this tedious winding duty.

Electrification of the lighthouse was the 20th century's most significant advance in lighting technology. High intensity electric lights, particularly the mercury vapor bulb, eliminated the need for elaborate ground glass prims and Fresnel lenses. Additionally batteries and solar power now have further streamlined illumination. Automation of all types of lights via computer is now standard practice although a few manned stations remain worldwide.

# Lighting America's Coast

The first lighthouse in the United States was built in 1716 on Little Brewster Island at the entrance to Boston Harbor to serve merchant and maritime interests in the Massachusetts colony. Candles or lamps burning whale oil produced the first light atop the circular tower with spider lamps installed in the 1790s. Although the acrid fumes produced by these oil-burning lamps burned the keeper's nostrils, limiting his time in the lantern room, this type of illumination was standard in American lighthouses until the introduction of Winslow Lewis' lighting system.

Ten additional lighthouses were built in the colonies prior to the Revolution; afterward the individual states maintained control of their respective lighthouses and made necessary repairs to damage inflicted by the war. In 1789 the US Lighthouse Service was established when Congress assigned national responsibility for maintenance and all activity relative to aids to navigation when the federal government was established. States were required to cede their lighthouses and all aids to navigation to the Treasury Department and signature of the President was required for appointment of keepers until the mid 1800s. Local superintendents retained responsibility for daily activities and operation of lighthouses, construction and repair, selection of sites for new structures, acquisition of the land and collection of customs. For these added duties they were compensated with 2.5 percent of all revenue related to lighthouses in their area.

The lighthouse at Portland Head (ME) was the first put into service following the Congressional act, followed by Cape Henry (VA) in 1792. Trade in the New England area thrived following the Revolution and a boom in lighthouse construction accompanied this growth. During the period 1800-1810, fourteen of nineteen lighthouses built were in New England and New York; only three of these were coastal lights, the rest harbor lights. To a lesser degree increased trade traffic also prompted construction of lighthouses in southern waters during the next decade, but New England still led the nation. Several additional coastal lights were built (inlcuding those on Boon and Petit Manan Islands), but most were again located in harbors or bays. By 1820 fifty five lighthouses were in operation along the east coast. As maritime trade increased, so did lighthouse construction. New structures were built at a steady rate throughout the late 1800s and into the early 1900s.

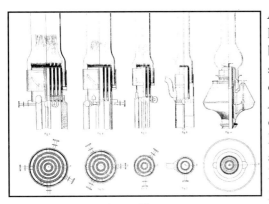
*Argand lamp*

As in Europe, oil lamps were used early on as illuminants for the light. These "spider" lamps consisted of a central oil reservoir (the body) and several projecting tubes (legs). Modeled after lighting systems used in England, the Argand lamp and parabolic reflector designed by Winslow Lewis became standard apparatus in early American lighthouses of the colonial period and early 1800s. Tests of this system at Boston Harbor light revealed the reflectors and lamps produced a light far superior to the spider lamps. Congress allotted $60,000 for purchase of Lewis' system, installation of the lights in all existing lighthouses and maintenance for a ten-year period. Lewis began installation in 1812, but was forced to interrupt his task during the War of 1812. He then completed the work in 1815 when fighting ceased. However, the lens used in the Argand lamps had a greenish tint which reduced the candlepower, a situation which had caused the British to abandon this system. Reflector shape was not uniform; many were not parabolic but spherical and were too thin and/or badly bent from repeated cleaning. However, the Lewis system was cost effective versus the Fresnel lens, so its use continued for roughly twenty years before the final switch.

By the late 1830s, the U. S. maritime community urged the government to adopt the Fresnel lens. In 1838 Congress sent Commodore Matthew Perry to Europe to purchase two of the lenses: one first-order fixed and one second-order flashing. These lenses were installed in the twin lights in Navesink, New Jersey and produced a light far superior to any other. Some 12 years later, when in need of repair, these lights were still noted to be of significantly better quality than nearby Sandy Hook which was equipped with the Lewis system. By the time of the Civil War, all lighthouses were fitted with Fresnel lenses and most had new lanterns. The largest lenses (first through third order) were considered suitable for coastal lights, with the smaller three orders installed in harbor or bay lights. A middle lens, 3.5 order, was developed later and used primarily in the Great Lakes lights.

Oil from the head of the sperm whale was the first fuel source for lens lamps in America's lighthouses. But, with a dramatic increase in the price of sperm oil between 1840 and early 1850s, another fuel source was sought. England and France were using colza, an oil made from rapeseed. The Lighthouse Board hoped that farmers would take note and begin to grow this plant, but they did not respond. Other options then had to be determined: lard oil was used for a time replaced later by kerosene about 1870. Although effective, the kerosene was extremely volatile and required careful handling. Typically a small, brick or stone building provided safe storage for the volatile oil. At the turn of the century, the incandescent oil vapor lamp came into use. Giving off a bright light, this lamp was used until electricity reached individual lighthouses--in some cases not until after World War II. The first light lit with electricity was the Statue of Liberty in 1886 which served as a "lighthouse" until 1903.

The 19th century also saw introduction of new materials and designs used in U.S. lighthouse construction. Cast iron structures became popular and a design using iron and wood in combination created pile lighthouses. The development of screwpile structures was particularly valuable as they could be built in the water on top of or near the navigational hazzard. A variation on the pile lighthouse, in which the iron piles, or legs, were driven into the sea bottom or set into rocks, was developed in the mid 1800s. The first pile lighthouse in the U.S. was constructed at Minots Ledge and went into service in 1850 but was blown over by a storm in 1852. Screwpile structures were built in the United States along the Chesapeake Bay, North Carolina sounds and the Gulf Coast. Each lighthouse had nine legs, one in the center with eight surrounding it in an octagonal arrangement; a platform was then built on top of the legs. The lighthouse, constructed on the flat surface, was a one-story dwelling for living quarters with lantern room and light on top.

*Screw pile Design*

In the late 1800s Caisson lighthouses, with concrete bases positioned securely on the sea bottom, were used extensively in the United States, particularly along the northern and mid-Atlantic coasts. Although the term "caisson" technically refers only to the bottom of the cylinder, typically the definition includes the entire cylindrical tube which is the foundation of the lighthouse. Because these sturdy structures readily withstood severe weather and bumps from passing vessels, they replaced lighthships stationed at sites that were too rough for bay screwpile or harbor lights.

Seven coastal tall towers were built during the 1850s (including those at Fire Island and Cape Hatteras), then another five in the 1870s and three in the 1880s. These structures, like earlier comparable structures, were made of brick. Often the US coastal lights were also painted with daymarks to differentiate them during daylight hours; most of these are seen along the Atlantic coast. Patterns are duplicated, but lights with identical markings are widely separated. By the turn of the century, an extensive system of navigational aids was in place along the US coasts, with the 1920s the heyday of lighthouses.

In 1851 Congress authorized a board to investigate the state of the country's navigational aids. The findings indicated that significant problems existed, among them poor management, towers too short for proper range, improper reflector shape, and poorly trained-to-incompetent keepers. The investigatory board noted a "better system" clearly was needed and recommended creation of a Lighthouse Board to manage the nation's lighthouses and other aids to navigation. Additionally, the plan called for establishment of lighthouse districts and installation of a Fresnel lens in all existing and new lighthouses. In 1852 the Lighthouse Board was officially established by Congress although it had commenced work well before that time.

The Board divided the country into twelve districts: two in the Great Lakes, seven along the Atlantic coast, two in the Gulf of Mexico and one for the West coast. As both the system and country grew, additional districts were added, finally totalling eighteen. An inspector managed each district; local customs collectors functioned as assistants, who typically hired and paid the keepers, and handled a variety of administrative duties. Gradually these assistants were phased out and the Lighthouse Board assigned an army engineer to each district. The district then had a naval officer (inspector) to ensure the lighthouses worked properly and that the keepers performed duties as required; the engineer (army officer) was responsible for construction, repair and maintenance.

Having brought order and improvement to the nation's aids to navigation, the Lighthouse Board was replaced in 1910 by the Lighthouse Bureau (or Lighthouse Service) as governing body. Congress enacted the change in order to instate civilian control of lighthouse matters. This organization was merged into the Coast Guard in 1939 and all individuals were given the choice of remaining civilian employees or joining the Coast Guard. By the mid 1900s advances in technology had created a sophisticated system to warn and guide mariners. The lightkeeper was gradually replaced by automated equipment and many lights were abandoned altogether. In the 1960s the process of automation of all U.S. lighthouses was undertaken; today only Boston Harbor light is staffed and will remain so to commemorate the historic significance of lighthouses and light keepers in maritime history.

## *Changing Roles: Looking Forward*

Today the lighthouse represents a symbol of maritime tradition and cultural history. With automation now standard and navigational technology often eliminating the need for particular lights entirely, other roles are being created for many of these locations, saving them from destruction, neglect and ruin. No longer simply left to fall victim to vandalism and the elements, lights which are no longer active navigational aids have taken on another important function. Local groups are restoring lighthouses in their area for use as tourist sites and interpretive centers so that future generations can learn about and, to some extent, relive a past era. Extensive preservation and reconstruction efforts are underway nationwide to return lighthouses to their former condition; those threatened by erosison are being relocated rather than being left to fall into the sea. The Maine Lights Program, an innovative program completed in 1998, saved numerous lighthouses and stations by assigning stewardship to local communities, private non-profit organizations, or appropriate State or Federal agencies. School children, visitors and local residents are now afforded access to many lighthouses nationwide and are then able to better appreciate the history they represent.

The few remaining lightkeepers (only at Boston Light in the U.S. and several throughout the Canadian provinces) also find their duties changing in light of continuing advances in technology. Time formerly spent polishing lenses, winding clockwork mechanisms and rescuing shipwreck victims is now used to interpret for visitors the spirit and history of the lightkeeping tradition. The changing role for lighthouses and the new "lightkeeper" ensures that the history represented by both will not fade.

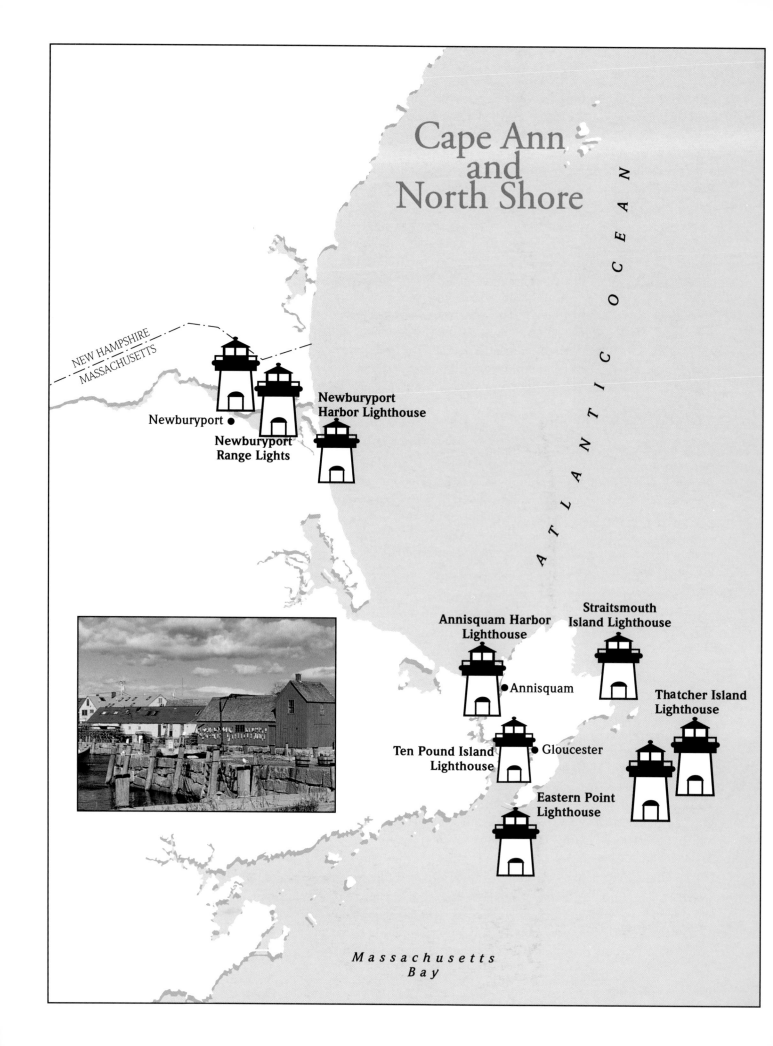

# Cape Ann and North Shore

ATLANTIC OCEAN

NEW HAMPSHIRE
MASSACHUSETTS

Newburyport •

**Newburyport Range Lights**

**Newburyport Harbor Lighthouse**

**Annisquam Harbor Lighthouse**

• Annisquam

**Straitsmouth Island Lighthouse**

**Ten Pound Island Lighthouse**

• Gloucester

**Thatcher Island Lighthouse**

**Eastern Point Lighthouse**

*Massachusetts Bay*

# The Massachusetts Lighthouse Tradition

*Compiled by Ted Panayotoff*

During the American Colonial period, a light station on Little Brewster Island in Boston Harbor was established by the Colony of Massachusetts in 1716. Destroyed by the British Army in 1776, the granite tower was not replaced until 1783. Massachusetts therefore boasts the first U.S. Lighthouse, but not the oldest continuously existing structure.  Other Colonial lighthouses were  Brant Point Light on Nantucket Island(1746), Plymouth Light on the Gurnet Point(1769) and Cape Ann Light on Thachers Island(1771).  All were replaced by later towers, with the present Brant Point tower the ninth lighthouse on the site.

Prior to the organization of the Federal Government and its assumption of responsibility for lighthouses in 1789,  the colony built two additional beacons, Great Point Light on Nantucket Island (1784), and Newburyport Harbor Light (1788).  Built of rubble stone, Great Point Light was destroyed by storm in 1884 but rebuilt two years later. The initial pair of range lights at Newburyport Harbor became a single light in 1856, replaced by the present wood tower in 1898.  During this period the destroyed Boston Light tower also was replaced with an 89-foot granite tower.

The U. S. Lighthouse Service, formed in 1789, became the Federal agency responsible for building and operating the  nation's lighthouses. Cape Cod Light at Truro (1797) was the first of 12 lighthouses along the Massachusetts coast built by the Service during a 20-year period. Of these, 11 stations remain with only the tower at Scituate (1811) the original structure. These early lighthouses were located primarily to mark Cape Cod and Martha's Vineyard-- Cape Cod (Highland) (1797), Chatham (1808) and Race Point (1816), Gay Head (1799) and Cape Poge(1802).

Most of the early lighthouses were of wood or rubble stone construction which, although cost effective, frequently required replacement due to deterioration or poor workmanship.  The replacement structures typically were  brick cylinders or cast iron towers.  An exception was Cape Poge Light, which retained its wood construction to facilitate the frequent moves required due to erosion.  During the next two decades, 16 more lighthouses were built to mark additional important harbors and hazards; 12 still exist as light stations with newer towers. Between 1839 and 1852  five more lighthouses were constructed. The original towers at Palmer Island (1849) in New Bedford Harbor and Sankaty Head Light on Nantucket (1850) still stand.  Also during this period, the first ill-fated Minots's Ledge Light was built to mark the dangerous ledge off  Cohasset.

One mandate of the Lighthouse Board, created in 1852, was to bring lighthouse structural design and construction under the supervision of trained civil engineers. With the exception Cleveland Ledge Light (1943), all the remaining Massachusetts lighthouses were built during the Lighthouse Board era, 1852 to 1905.   In the early 1850s, the Board began the use of standard tower designs: brick cylinders of varying height, tapered square brick towers and, by the 1870's, widespread use of cast iron.   Nine cast iron towers with brick lining were built between 1873 and 1881; seven exist today (Chatham, Race Point, Nauset, Nobska , East Chop and Edgartown). Three small cast iron towers and three cast iron caisson towers were built between 1871 and 1898: Fort Pickering and Ten Pound Island (small towers), Duxbury Pier and Butler Flats (caisson). The cast iron skeleton tower at Marblehead, built in 1896, is unique to Massachusetts but common to other areas.  Brick was used to construct towers at Eastern Point (1890), West Chop (1891), Annisquam (1897) Hospital Point (1871), Wood End(1872) and Long Point (1875). Perhaps the most "classic" lighthouse construction, the granite tower, was used at Boston Light (1783), Graves Light(1905), Baker's Island (1821), Cape Ann /Thacher's Island (1861) and Minot's Ledge Light (1860), well known for it's 1-4-3 characteristic, making it the "I Love You Light".

Because  it includes the first, and one of the last, lighthouses built in the United States, Massachusetts has a vivid lighthouse tradition. Particular care has been taken to preserve the lights as a valuable element of  the state's compelling maritime history.

# Newburyport Harbor Range Lights

*Front Range Light*

The range lights were first built in 1873 to help mariners entering Newburyport Harbor from the Merrimac River. The Front Range light originally was an octagonal wooden tower located on Bayley's Wharf. The Rear Range light is a 53-foot brick tower with cast-iron lantern room and balcony. The lighthouse is square with some tapering in the midsection.

These lights were discontinued in 1961 and in 1964 the Front Range light was moved to the nearby grounds of a Coast Guard Station. In 1990 it was changed to a more traditional appearance with short, white tower and red and white lantern room. After decommissioning, the Rear Range light was sold to private ownership. Both lights are listed on the National Register of Historic Places.

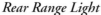

*Rear Range Light*

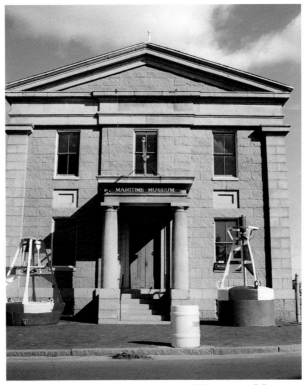

*Maritime Museum*

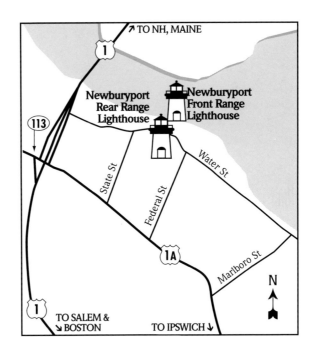

**Directions:** Newburyport can be reached by taking I-95 to Exit 57 and following Rt. 133 east to "Downtown Newburyport" or via Routes 1 and 1A. Signs indicating the Historic/Downtown area are easily followed. Any of several cross streets will lead to Water Street (Broad, State, Federal are examples).

The front range light is located inside the U.S. Coast Guard Merrimack River Station on Water St. between Federal and Tremont streets. Parking is available behind the building. The rear range tower is on Water Street, just south of the Coast Guard Station and is easily identified once in the area.

# Newburyport Harbor (Plum Island) Light

Shifting channels at the mouth of the Merrimack River made entrance to Newburyport harbor difficult and dangerous in the 18th century, prompting local merchants to pay for construction of two wooden lighthouses at the northern tip of Plum Island in 1787. The lighthouses were ceded to the federal government in 1790 with the first keeper appointed by George Washington. The original towers were built on moveable foundations to they could be easily relocated as the sandbars around Plum Island shifted. By lining up the two range lights mariners knew they were following the best channel into the harbor.

In 1838 the lighthouses were replaced by a pair of octagonal towers, again on moveable foundations. A strange-looking small tower called the "Bug Light" was added in 1855; one of the lighthouses was destroyed by fire in 1856 but not rebuilt. The surviving lighthouse received a fourth-order Fresnel lens.

Shifting sands left the remaining tower and "Bug" too far inland, necessitating relocation several times between 1870 and 1898. Finally, in 1898, a new 45-foot wooden tower was built and the lens from the old light installed. The light was automated in 1951 and the Fresnel lens removed in 1981.

C. 1916

The lighthouse now stands on the grounds of the Parker River National Wildlife Refuge headquarters; the tower is leased from the Coast Guard to the New England Lighthouse Foundation. Plans call for restoration of the tower's interior and conversion of the keeper's house into a museum.

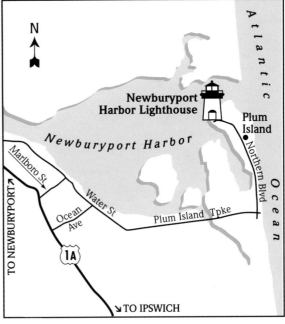

**Directions:** From I-95, take Exit 57 (Historic Newburyport) to Rt 113 into Newburyport (or from Rt 1, exit to Downtown Newburyport). Take one of the main cross streets(Broad, Federal, State) north to Water Street (most all cross streets will take you there). Follow Water Street east to a T-intersection with Ocean Avenue. A sign indicating Plum Island & Parker River Refuge is to the left. Continue straight on the Plum Island Turnpike; turn left onto Northern Blvd. and follow this road to its end at the Parker River National Wildlife Refuge.
**Or:** Take MA 1A North to Newbury. At the first traffic light, turn right onto Ocean Avenue(a "Plum Island" directs you). Follow Ocean Avenue to its end at a T-intersection with Plum Island Turnpike and turn right; there is a sign indicating Parker River Refuge. Follow above directions to the lighthouse.

# Annisquam Light

The present Annisquam Light, also known as "Squam Light" and "Wigwam Light", is the third at this location. In 1801 the United States government bought the property from the Commonwealth of Massachusetts for $140.00. A wooden tower and wood-framed keeper's house were built; the house still stands with some modifications. The stone oil house built at that time also survives. By the 1820s the lighthouse was in poor condition, propped up with poles for a time. In 1851 a new octagonal, 40-foot wooden tower was built and a fifth-order Fresnel lens added in 1856.

A new 41-foot Federal-style brick tower was built in 1897 and in 1922 the kerosene-fueled light and fifth order lens were removed, replaced by an electrified fourth-order lens. The new light increased Annisquam Light's brightness from 1,300 to 250,000 candlepower. A fog signal was added in 1965; the lighthouse was automated in 1974.

Edward L. Hopper was born at this lighthouse in 1879, where his father was keeper from 1872-1894. In a letter he described a shipwreck which occurred around 1890. The *Abbie B. Cramer*, a three-masted coal schooner from Baltimore, went ashore at the west end of Coffin's Beach, now called Wingaersheek Beach. All hands had to stay in the vessel's rigging awaiting help. Rescuers carried a lifeboat two miles across sand to reach the wreck and rescue the crew. Hopper claimed that years later he could see wood from the schooner protruding from the sand at low tide.

A Coast Guard family now lives at the light station. There is a small parking area, but the lighthouse is not open to the public.

### Directions:

From MA 127 (from Rockport or Gloucester) turn onto Leonard Rd.; this intersection is about 3 miles from the Grant Circle intersection of MA 128 and MA 127 and 1 mile from Plum Beach Cove Beach. At a "Norwood Heights" sign, turn right onto Elizabeth Rd. (about 0.3 mile). Cross Ocean Ave. to the intersection with Harraden Circle; turn right toward the harbor. Turn right, then left onto Lighthouse Rd. (0.7mile). The lighthouse is at the end of Lighthouse Rd. with a small parking area for "lighthouse viewing". Roads are not all marked.Tour boats out of Gloucester also offer good views.

*Annisquam Harbor, circa 1904*

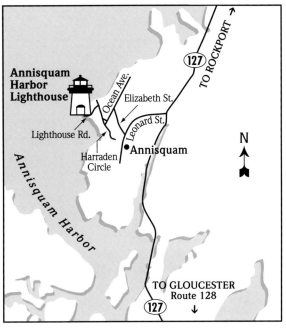

# Thacher Island Lights  (Thatchers, Cape Ann)

Thachers Island, off Rockport on Cape Ann, was named by Anthony Thacher, an Englishman whose fishing vessel, the *Watch and Wait*, was wrecked near the island in 1635. Thacher and his wife, Elizabeth, were the only survivors of the wreck in which 21 people died; Thacher was awarded the island to recompense him for his losses.

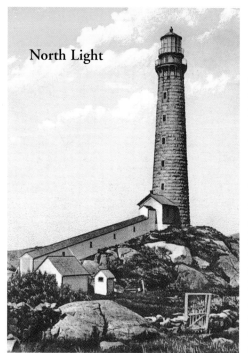

**North Light**

In 1771 there were only three lighthouses in operation north of Cape Cod: Boston, Plymouth and Portsmouth. To this point, lighthouses were built to mark port entrances; the construction of twin towers on Thachers Island in 1771 marked the first such lights to mark a "dangerous spot." Two 45-foot stone towers, about 300 yards apart, were lighted for the first time on December 21, 1771; the station was ceded to the federal government in 1790.

**South Light**

The lights at Thacher Island were the first seen by many coming from Europe into Massachusetts Bay. In 1810 the south tower became the second lighthouse (after Boston) to receive a new Argand lamp and parabolic reflector. A new stone house was built in 1816 (it still stands) and a fog bell installed in 1853. New, taller (124 foot) towers were built in 1861 with Fresnel lenses installed in each.

On December 21, 1864 keeper Alexander Bray left for the mainland to take an ailing assistant keeper to the doctor. His wife, Maria, and 14-year-old nephew Sidney Haskell were left at the light station. Later that day a heavy snow storm swept the area, making it impossible for Bray to return to the island.

**North Light**

"Thacher Island Twin Lights
Rockport, Massachusetts
has been placed on the National Register
of Historic Places by the
United States Department of the Interior
October 7, 1971"

**South Light**

24

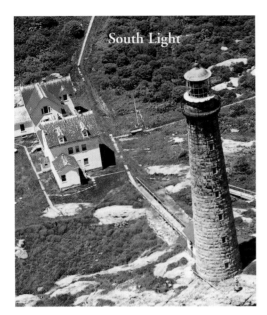

South Light

South Light

For two nights Maria Bray and Sidney Haskell braved high winds and heavy snow to light the lamps in both towers; each tower had 148 steps with three trips needed to keep the lamps filled with oil and lantern room panes free of soot.

In 1932 the north light was extinguished and the south light intensified to 70,000 candlepower. The south light and fog signal were automated in 1980. Concerned citizens of Cape Ann formed the Thachers Island Association and chose a caretaker to live on the island. In 1989 the north light was restored and opened to visitors. There are no longer caretakers on the island; the boat ramp was washed away in the winter of 1995. The lightstation was designated a National Historic Landmark in 2001. Views are possible from shore or from tour boats.

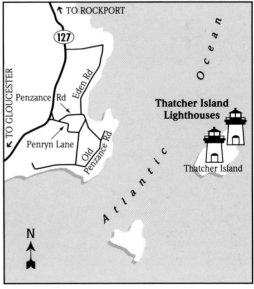

**Directions:**
The twin lighthouses are visible in the distance from along MA 127A. For clearer views, turn east at the South Street-Thacher Rd. signs (1.5 miles north of the "Entering Rockport" sign or 1.2 miles south of Marmion Way in Rockport). There is a "triangle" at the intersection. At Penzance Rd. turn left and continue to Old Penzance Rd. Turn left onto Old Penzance Rd. which becomes a dirt road. There is an open field for parking at the road's end. A good view of the lighthouses is possible from the rocky knoll known as Loblolly Knoll. For a time the Thachers Island Association offered trips to the island. However landing is now impossible after a 1995 storm washed out the boat ramp. The lighthouses are best photographed by boat.

# Straitsmouth Island Light

Rockport's vital granite business began in the 1820s and, together with the already flourishing fishing industry, put the town on the map. Straitsmouth Island light was built in 1835 to assist mariners with entry into the harbor at nearby Pigeon Cove. Several vessels were lost in storms in the 1830s and 1840s in the vicinity of the island, prompting placement of a warning buoy near Avery's Rock nearby.

In the 1850s a new Fresnel lens was installed and in 1896 the present 37-foot brick tower built to replace the old one. The light was converted from white to green in 1932, automated in 1967 and the Fresnel lens subsequently removed. The island was sold to private ownership in 1941, but was eventually acquired by the Massachusetts Audubon Society; the property is now part of the Ipswich Wildlife Sanctuary.

The 1835 wooden keeper's house still stands but is currently boarded up and in disrepair. Although the old entryway to the tower was destroyed by a storm in October, 1991, it has since been replaced; an oil house also remains. The lighthouse can be seen in the distance from the breakwater at the end of Bearskin Neck in Rockport or from some of the excursion cruises in the area.

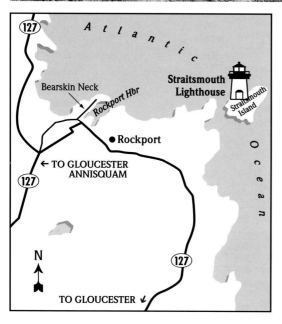

**Directions:**
The lighthouse is located at the entrance to Rockport Harbor and can be seen at a distance from the end of Bearskin Neck (pedestrian area which ends at the breakwater). Rockport is reached from MA 127/127A from North or South; it is a congested area with limited parking near the waterfront. The wharf is the site of the much-photographed and painted Motif #1 (harbor, lobster boats). The lighthouse is best photographed by boat.

# Ten Pound Island Light

Ten Pound Island, in Gloucester harbor, achieved notoriety in 1817 when several people reported seeing a large sea serpent on the ledges on the island's eastern side. Among the witnesses was Amos Story. In 1821 a 40-foot stone lighthouse, keeper's house and oil house were built and Mr. Story, the sea serpent descriptor, became the first keeper in 1833. A new 30-foot cast-iron tower, lined with brick, was built in 1881

Over the years, the island has hosted a fish hatchery, artist Winslow Homer and a Coast Guard air station intended to catch rum runners during prohibition. In 1956 Ten Pound Island light was decommissioned and the fifth-order Fresnel lens removed; the new optic was put on the old bell tower, then later moved to a skeleton tower. The house and outbuildings had been reduced to rubble. Ownership of the island reverted to the town of Gloucester.

The Lighthouse Preservation Society initiated restoration of the lighthouse in the 1980s, with federal and private funds obtained. The tower was repaired and the automatic light returned. Ten Pound Island light was relighted as an active aid to navigation on August 7, 1989; the oil house was restored in 1995. The light can be seen from many points along the Gloucester waterfront or from tour boats.

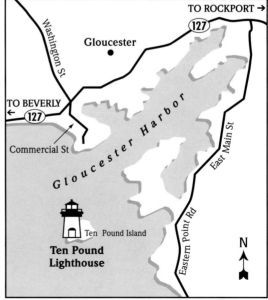

**Directions:**
The light can be seen from Pavilion Beach Park on MA 127 (Main St.) about 1 mile west of the Washington and Commercial intersection and just east of the draw bridge in Gloucester. A small beach area immediately outside the entrance to the Eastern Point area also offers distant views. Excursion boat trips from Gloucester offer the best views and pass by several other lighthouses as well.

# Eastern Point Light

The first stone lighthouse tower at Eastern Point, completed in 1832, was intended to aid fishermen and mariners entering Gloucester Harbor. This light assumed new importance with the arrival of the railroad and subsequent increase in fishing business. A new 34-foot lighthouse was built in 1848; its revolving light was turned by a clockwork mechanism wound periodically by the keeper. A fog bell also was operated by similar mechanism.

The present (third) Eastern Point Light was built in 1890 on the old foundation of the 1832 tower. The 36-foot brick lighthouse, attached to the keeper's house by covered walkway, received a fourth-order Fresnel lens. This lens was removed in 1919 and replaced by a rotating aerobeacon. The two-story duplex house that still stands was built in 1879; the oil house survives from 1894. The garage and fog signal are more recent, built in 1947 and 1951 respectively. At the end of the 2,250-foot breakwater there is a strictly utilitarian light, marking the dangerous Dog Bar Reef. Both lights were automated in 1986.

The Coast Guard made repairs to the station in 1993 and a Coast Guard family now lives in the keeper's house. There is a parking area at the station but the grounds are closed to the public. You can walk along the breakwater for excellent views of the lighthouse. Tour boats from Gloucester also pass the light as do seasonal special cruises from Hull or Boston Harbor.

*Gloucester Breakwater Light*

C. 1907

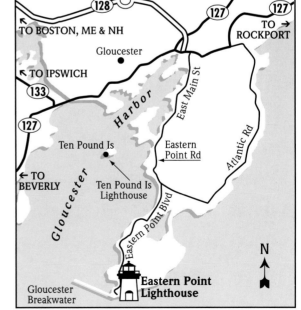

**Directions:** From Rt 128 in Gloucester follow East Main St. to Niles Beach and the entrance to Eastern Point at Eastern Point Boulevard West. This road leads through an exclusive residential area marked with "Residents Only" and "Private" signs. The road is a public right-of-way and visitors are allowed to drive directly to the lighthouse. There is a parking area at the lighthouse with good views from that area and along the granite breakwater. The tour boats out of Gloucester also offer good photo opportunities.

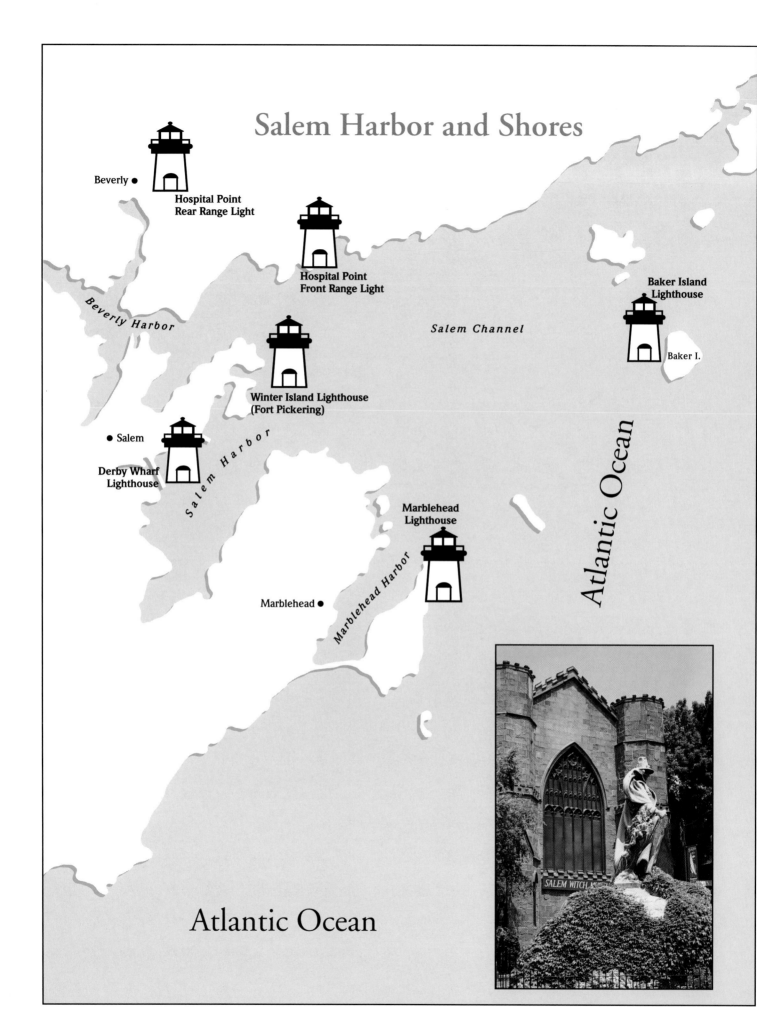

# Salem Harbor and Shores

Beverly ●

**Hospital Point
Rear Range Light**

**Hospital Point
Front Range Light**

*Beverly Harbor*

*Salem Channel*

**Baker Island
Lighthouse**

Baker I.

**Winter Island Lighthouse
(Fort Pickering)**

● Salem

**Derby Wharf
Lighthouse**

*Salem Harbor*

*Atlantic Ocean*

**Marblehead
Lighthouse**

Marblehead ●

*Marblehead Harbor*

SALEM WITCH

Atlantic Ocean

# Derby Wharf Light

For many years the twin lights at Bakers Island had sufficed to guide vessels into Salem Harbor, but it was decided another light was needed to help mariners find their way into the crowded inner harbor. The unusual 12-foot square, 25-foot tall brick lighthouse was built and put into service in 1871. Because of proximity to the city, Derby Wharf light always had a caretaker rather than resident keeper.

The original fifth-order Fresnel was changed in 1906 to a fourth-order with flashing red light. In 1910 reclassification to a harbor light required replacement with a sixth-order lens (reverting to fixed light). The light was automated in the 1970s, then deactivated in 1977 with ownership going to the National Park Service. In 1983 the Friends of Salem Maritime had Derby Wharf relighted as a private aid to navigation with solar-powered optic. The wharf dates back to the 1760s and is part of the Salem National Historic Park. The Customs House where Nathaniel Hawthorne worked is across the street and the House of Seven Gables nearby.

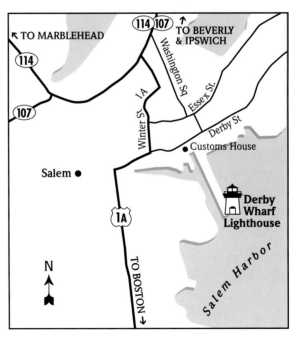

**Directions:** Follow MA 1A, 114 or 107 into Salem. Turn east onto Derby Street (Derby St. is also reached by following Washington Square east from MA 1A or Fort Avenue from Winter Island). The lighthouse is at the end of the wharf opposite the restored Customs House and about three blocks from the House of Seven Gables.

# Winter Island (Fort Pickering) Light

Winter Island light, also known as Fort Pickering Light, was built in 1871, along with Derby Wharf and Hospital Point lights. With the addition of these new lights, mariners would line up Winter Island and Derby Wharf lights after passing Bakers Island on the way into Salem harbor. The lighthouse was built of iron lined with brick and exhibited a flashing white light 28 feet above sea level. The island was the site of 18th century Fort Pickering, much of which still stands; several 19th century hangings were held at the island's Gallows Hill and the grounds served as a militia training ground.

A Coast Guard airplane hanger was located on Winter Island in 1934 with Coast Guard personnel living in the old keeper's house while new quarters were built. The keeper's house and outbuildings were later removed. The lighthouse was deactivated in 1969 and fell into disrepair. A group of concerned citizens saved the lighthouse and it was relighted in 1983 as a private aid to navigation, then converted to solar power in 1994.

*Fort Pickering, Winter Island*

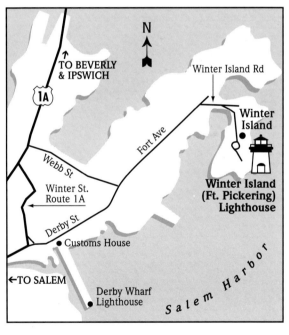

**Directions:**
Take MA 1A into Salem; turn left (south) at Webb St. Bear left (east) at Fort Avenue, then right at Winter Island Road ("Winter Island Marine Recreation Area" sign). From Salem, follow 1A to Derby Street/Fort Avenue then continue to Winter Island Road and the entrance to the park. There are a variety of ways to enter the Salem area; directional signs to Winter Island are posted frequently to guide you.

# Hospital Point Range Lights

Like neighboring Salem, Beverly was an active port for both trade and fishing in the 18th and 19th centuries. Hospital Point, Derby Wharf and Fort Pickering Lighthouses all were built in 1871 to guide vessels into the harbors. The 45-foot Federal-style lighthouse is located at the former site of a smallpox hospital, the area having become known as "hospital point". The two-story keeper's house still stands, with major additions in 1968 almost surrounding the actual lighthouse. The original oil house also remains.

Hospital Point light still has the original 3 1/2- order Fresnel lens with condensing panel in front. This panel, considered unique to American lighthouses, causes the light intensity to diminish as the mariner veers from the main channel into Salem Harbor.

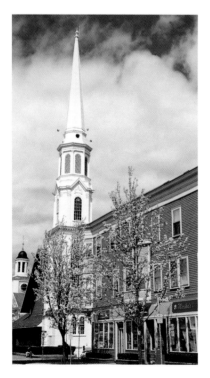

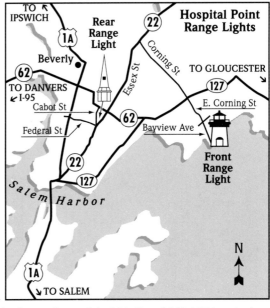

In 1927 the light officially became Hospital Point Range Front Light; a rear range light was placed in the steeple of the First Baptist Church one mile away. The steeple light is aligned with the front range light to further guide vessels into Salem Harbor. Automated in 1947, this lighthouse has since been home to the Commander of the First Coast Guard District. The lighthouse is easily accessible but grounds are not open. At dead low tide walking from nearby Ober Street Beach takes you in front of the lighthouse.

**Directions:**
In Beverly, turn east from MA 127 onto East Corning Street (approximately 0.4 miles northeast of the MA 62 and MA 127 junction). Bear left at Bayview Ave. and continue to the road's end in a cul-de-sac and the front range light. At low tide it is possible to walk around the beach from Lynch Park to get a front view of the light. At the intersection of Neptune/Ober St. and East Corning, turn right and continue bearing right to Ober St. The park is to the left. The rear range light is located in steeple of the First Baptist Church located at the intersection of Cabot, Federal and Dane Streets.

# Bakers Island Light

At the entrance to Salem Harbor, Bakers Island was first annexed to Salem in 1630 and has long been home to summer residents. In 1791, a day marker was placed on the island. Because this was inadequate for the increased shipping traffic in the area, Congress authorized the construction of twin lighthouses on Bakers Island. The first Bakers Island lights were lit on January 3, 1798 with the two towers located atop the keeper's house, at either end of the building.

For a time one of Bakers Island's twin lights was extinguished. Mariners claimed this made it difficult to distinguish this light from Boston Light and an increased number of wrecks attested to the confusion. New towers were subsequently built and lighted in 1821. One of the towers was slightly taller than the other leading to the nickname "Mr. & Mrs. Light-houses". The taller light received a fourth-order Fresnel lens in 1855.

When, in 1907, a new air siren replaced the old fog bell at the lighthouse, complaints of the island residents were vehement. The signal was then redirected toward the sea through a megaphone so that it was barely audible on the island. In 1916 the smaller lighthouse was discontinued and subsequently torn down. At that time the taller tower received an acetylene-powered lamp;it now houses a modern plastic optic.The light was automated in 1972.

In 1887 Dr. Nathan Morse of Salem bought the entire island, except the lighthouse and station. He built a large health spa, the Winne-egan and proclaimed the Bakers Island air "highly charged with ozone from the ocean". Former President Benjamin Harrison and Actress Lillian Russell were among visitors to Bakers Island in the Winne-egan heyday.

The spa burned in 1906. Bakers Island still has a sizable summer colony, despite tales of ghostly hauntings. Today, the island is managed by the Bakers Island Association, founded in 1914.

C. 1907

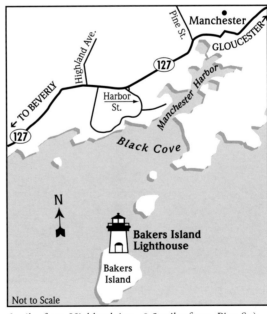

**Directions:**
From MA 127 in Manchester-by-the-Sea, turn east onto Harbor Street ( about .6 miles from Highland Ave., 0.5 miles from  Pine St.). Bear right as the road narrows into an exclusive residential area.  The view of the lighthouse from the beach is distant and binoculars are required. The best views are obtained by boat; excursion trips run by Boston Harbor Explorers, Friends of Boston Harbor Islands and others pass this light.

# Marblehead Light

Over the years many have noted how much more scenic the picturesque harbor would be if Marblehead Light was a traditional white lighthouse instead of a metal skeleton tower. Edward Rowe Snow wrote "..it is to be realized that lighthouses are for utility and not for beauty, but in this case it is especially unfortunate that beauty and utility were not combined."

The first lighthouse in the part of Marblehead Neck known as Point O'Neck was of the traditional style: white tower attached to keeper's house with covered walkway. However, with the growing popularity of Marblehead Neck as a summer resort, large "cottages" sprung up around the lighthouse, obscuring it from view from the sea.

The present structure, built in 1895, was intended to ensure visibility. Composed of eight cast-iron pilings connected by supports, the tower includes a spiral stairway with 105 steps leading to the lantern room. The keeper's house is gone, but a brick oil house still stands. Past requests from town officials to paint the structure white obviously have been unsuccessful as the tower remains a "military brown."

Point Light, Marblehead Neck, Mass.

The light originally was fitted with a Fresnel lens, exhibiting a steady white light; this characteristic was later changed to red, then green making Marblehead the only such light on the coast. The light was automated in 1960 and a plastic optic installed. Lighthouse grounds are now a park area.

### Marblehead Light

*"Est. 1882...By permission of congress..Original stone lighthouse was replaced by present structure of iron in 1888...130 ft above sea level...visibility app. 20 miles..First keeper of the light was Ezekiel Darling, a gunner in the old frigate constelation.."*

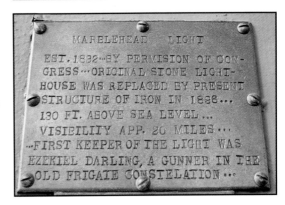

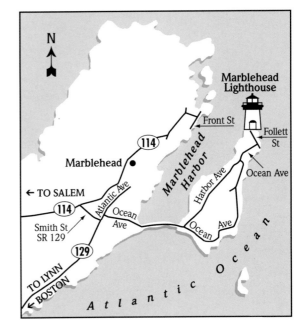

**Directions:** Follow MA 114 into Marblehead from Salem or MA 129 from Lynn. Turn east onto Ocean Avenue and cross a causeway, bearing left into Harbor Avenue. Reconnect with Ocean Avenue at follow it to its end at Follett Street (one way). Continue into Chandler Hovey Park. The light tower can also be seen at a distance from Front Street in Marblehead by following MA 114 to its end and continuing to the town wharf.

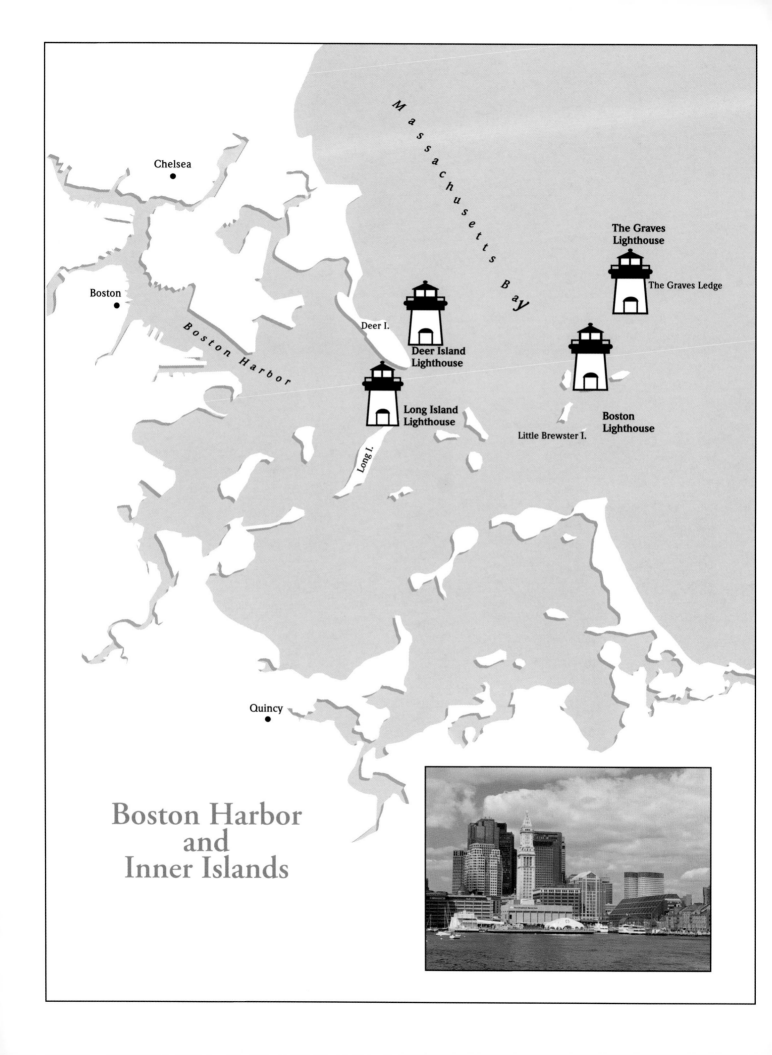

Chelsea

Boston

*Massachusetts Bay*

Deer I.

Deer Island
Lighthouse

Boston Harbor

Long Island
Lighthouse

Long I.

The Graves
Lighthouse

The Graves Ledge

Boston
Lighthouse

Little Brewster I.

Quincy

Boston Harbor
and
Inner Islands

# Boston Light

Called the "ideal American lighthouse" by historian Edward Rowe Snow, Boston light holds an honored place among lighthouses. It was the first lighthouse built in North America and is the only one in the United States today which has not been automated. Because the lighthouse was destroyed in the Revolution and rebuilt in 1783, the tower itself is the nation's second oldest.

Because Boston was the maritime center of colonial America, there were lighted beacons in the area before Boston light, but these were only lanterns on poles. In 1713 a Boston merchant representing the city's business community proposed a lighthouse to mark the entrance to the harbor; on July 23, 1715 the Boston Light Bill was passed. A stone tower was then built on Little Brewster Island, financed by a one-cent-per-ton tax on all vessels entering or leaving the harbor. The light was placed in service September 14, 1716 by the first keeper, George Worthylake. Several fires did substantial damage to the lighthouse tower during the 18th century, some apparently caused by lightening. However, a lightening rod was never put on the tower as it was thought that such a device would go against the will of God.

*Photo by John Forbes*

41

# Boston Light

In July 1775, with Boston Harbor under British control, American troops were sent to the island where they burned parts of the tower. The British immediately began repairing the lighthouse, but American soldiers again landed and were easy victors over the British guard; the lighthouse was again burned. At the close of the Revolution the British lingered in Boston harbor for some months. When leaving the area in June of 1776, troops set off a timed charge on Little Brewster Island, completely destroying the lighthouse. The remains of the metal lantern were used to make ladles for American cannons.

Reconstruction of Boston light wasn't completed until 1783. The new 75-foot tall rubblestone tower was built on order of John Hancock, then governor of Massachusetts, and became property of the federal government in 1789. In 1859 the light was raised to its present height of 89 feet. A new lantern room was added to house a 12-sided, second-order Fresnel lens which revolved on machinery run by a clockwork mechanism. A keeper's duplex was also built during that year, then a second keeper's house added in 1885 to accommodate the three keepers assigned to the light. In the 1930s 16 children among the three keepers' families were at home on one-acre Little Brewster Island.

# Boston Light

The Coast Guard took over operation of Boston light in 1941. During World War II the light was extinguished, then brought back into operation in July 1945. The light was electrified in 1948 and an electric motor replaced the clockwork mechanism that rotated the lens; the original Fresnel lens remains in place, visible for 27 miles. In 1960 the duplex keepers' house was burned.

Coast Guard staff now alternate two-week duty rotations on the island, often accompanied by an animal companion. A mutt named Farah lived on Little Brewster for 13 years and a recent frisky black feline resident was named Ida Lewis, after America's most famous woman lighthouse keeper. The gravestone of Farah, "beloved mutt" can be seen near the lighthouse. Odd happenings also have been reported at the station: a radio mysteriously changing channels from rock to classical and the figure of a man sitting in the lantern room seen by a recent keeper when he and his assistant were the only ones on the island.

**Directions:**

Friends of Boston Harbor Islands and the Boston Harbor Explorers schedule excursions which offer close views of the light and, in some cases, landing on the island for a brief visit. **Friends of Boston Harbor Island Boat Trips, 349 Lincoln St.- Bldg 45, Hingham, MA 02114 (617) 740-4290. Boston Harbor Explorers P.O. Box 744, Quincy, MA. 02269 (617) 479-1871**

# Boston Light

Boston light was named a National Historic Landmark in 1964, one of three lighthouses to receive this designation. The light was scheduled for automation in 1989, completing the process of automating all United States lighthouses. Preservation groups appealed and funding was appropriated to keep Coast Guard staff on the island, operating the light and other equipment as a living museum of lighthouse history. Meteorological data and daily positions of 25 navigational aids are recorded.

Recent storms have done serious damage to the island and, despite erosion control measures, Boston light will eventually be threatened by the sea. In 1990 a Stewardship Plan and preservation guidelines for the island and light were commissioned. As a result of that study, much recent work has been done on the island, including the keeper's house and outbuildings. Friends of Boston Harbor Islands offers trips to Little Brewster Island each summer; names of visitors dating back to the 18th century can be seen carved into the rocks and the view of Boston harbor is breathtaking.

# Deer Island Light

No more than a light on a fiberglass pole, the present Deer Island Light is built strictly with utility in mind. The light is located south of the Town of Winthrop, about 500 yards from Deer Island. The island itself has an unpleasant past as an internment camp for Indians, site of a state prison and immigrant quarantine station; a sewage treatment plant is now on the island.

The first Deer Island light was a sparkplug-type, built in 1890to mark a treacherous sandbar and to indicate the ship channel along President Roads into Boston Harbor. Painted brown, the old lighthouse has been described as a three-tier wedding cake with chocolate frosting.

Several particularly notable tales are associated with this light. The most tragic incident took place in 1916. The keeper, Joseph McCabe, left the lighthouse to meet his fiancee on Deer Island to address wedding invitations.  Ice around the lighthouse trapped McCabe's boat, so he decided to walk across the sandbar. Nearing the island, he lost his

footing and disappeared into the ocean, drowning in the icy waves. Tom Small became keeper in 1931, bringing with him a cat that gained fame as the "climbing cat of Deer Island Light." Reportedly, Small's cat would leap into the water, emerge with a fish, climb the ladder and eat the catch. Finally, it seems that during the days of prohibition, the keepers were illegally brewing malt liquor at the lighthouse. When an inspector arrived without notice the enterprise was abruptly put to rest.

By the early 1980s Deer Island light had deteriorated to the point of being unsafe. In 1982, much to the surprise and dismay of area residents, the iron lighthouse was removed and replaced by a 51-foot fiberglass, matchstick-like modular tower set on the original caisson.

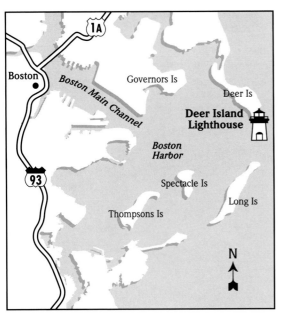

**Directions:** Excursion boats from Boston will pass this light, although at varying distances; trips with Friends of Boston Harbor Islands or  Boston Harbor Explorers are examples. The light can also be seen at a distance from the shore on Winthrop Beach in Winthrop, MA.

# Graves Light

A new major shipping channel into Boston Harbor (Broad Sound Channel), which opened in the early 20th century, necessitated the building of a lighthouse at the ledges called the Graves. The ledges were named in the 1600s for Thomas Graves, Vice-Admiral of Governor Winthrop's Navy.

The building of the 113-foot Graves light took place from 1903 to 1905. Granite for the light was cut at Rockport, MA.. Rock on the ledges was blasted and the foundation laid just four feet above the low tide mark. When it went into service, the Graves Light was measured at 380,000 candlepower with a first-order Fresnel lens. The light was later upgraded to 3.2 million candlepower, and for many years was the most powerful along the New England coast.

The keepers lived in the third, fourth and fifth stories, with the entrance to the lighthouse at the top of a 40-foot ladder. A water cistern was filled twice each year by a lighthouse tender; in addition to regular food deliveries, keepers augmented their diet with lobsters from traps they tended around the ledges.

Noted among the several wrecks in the vicinity of Graves Light was the *City of Salisbury* in 1938, remembered as the "Zoo Ship" for its cargo of zoo animals. The ship struck a reef close to the Graves, but no lives were lost and she became a tourist attraction for a few months before splitting in two and sinking.

Storms have destroyed the walkway and vandals have caused thousands of dollars in damage to the lighthouse; the fog signal was swept away by the "No-Name Storm" of October, 1991. The landing platform was repaired in 1993 and the original oil house still stands. The Graves Light was automated in 1976. Its Fresnel lens, 12 feet high and nine feet in diameter, is in storage at the Smithsonian Institution. The light was converted to solar power in 2001.

### Directions:
The light is best viewed by boat; Friends of Boston Habor Islands and Harbor Explorers both offer trips which pass this lighthouse.

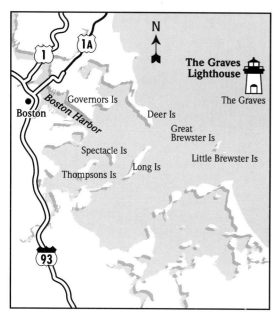

# Long Island Head Light

The longest island in Boston Harbor, Long Island has been home to a resort hotel, military fortifications and a hospital. Legend has it that the island is haunted by the "Woman in Scarlet", the ghost of the wife of a British solider killed by cannon fire in 1776 and buried on the island. In 1819 the first stone lighthouse tower was built on a hill on Long Island Head to guide vessels entering the harbor. The site is second only to Boston Light as the harbor's oldest light station, sometimes referred to as Inner Harbor Light.

In the 1850s, a 3-1/2 order Fresnel lens was installed, then a new 52-foot brick lighthouse constructed about 1900 to make room for enlargement of the island's fortification, Fort Strong. This was the third lighthouse on Long Island Head; construction date of the second tower is uncertain.

The last keeper, Edwin Tarr, died while sitting in his chair, looking out at the harbor. While the funeral in the keeper's house was ongoing, a sleet storm covered the hill with ice. When attempting to carry the casket down the path, a pallbearer slipped, losing his grip and sending the coffin sliding downhill. Seeing no other recourse, the men threw themselves on the moving casket, toboggan style, and managed to arrest it just at the head of the wharf.

After being discontinued in 1982, a solar-powered optic was installed, the tower renovated and the light reactivated in 1985. The keeper's house and outbuildings no longer remain. Although there is a bridge to the island to provide access to other buildings, entrance is closely guarded and visiting the lighthouse not permitted. A variety of boats out of Boston Harbor pass this lighthouse.

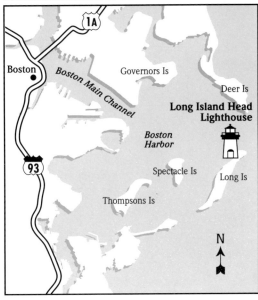

**Directions:** All boats from Long Wharf to George's Island pass Long Island Head; there are 5-6 departures daily during summer months. Any excursion boat from Rowe's or Long Wharf will pass this light, although the views vary in distance.

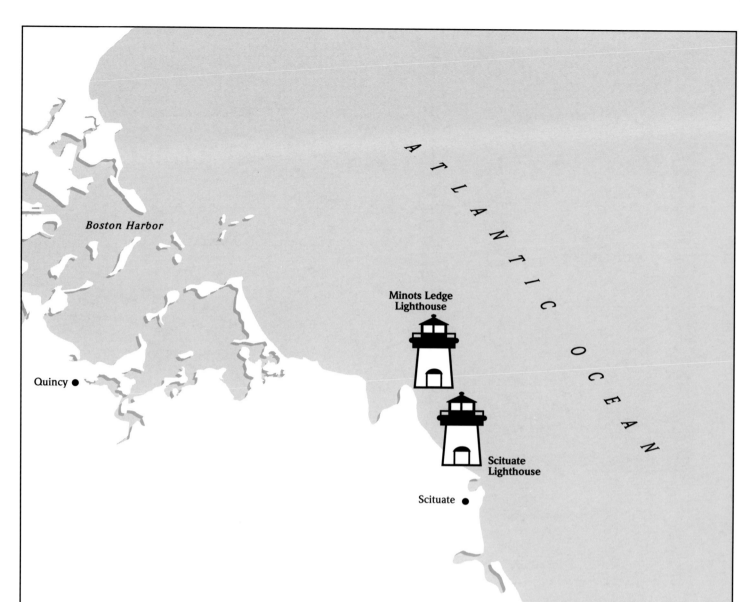

Boston Harbor

Quincy ●

A T L A N T I C   O C E A N

**Minots Ledge Lighthouse**

**Scituate Lighthouse**

Scituate ●

# The South Shore

Duxbury ●

**Plymouth Lighthouse (The Gurnet)**

**Duxbury Pier Lighthouse**

Plymouth ●

# Duxbury Pier Light

Built in 1871 on the north side of the main channel in Plymouth Harbor, this lighthouse marks the dangerous shoal off Saquish Head. The unusual coffeepot-shaped lighthouse is known locally as "Bug Light" or "The Bug". There are three levels which were used as living quarters; the lantern room held a fourth-order Fresnel lens.

The light was automated in 1965 and during the next two decades fell victim to vandalism. In 1983, with Duxbury Pier light slated for replacement with a tower similar to that of Deer Island, a group of local residents formed Project Bug Light. The group convinced the Coast Guard to alter those plans and a five-year lease was granted to the preservation committee. The Coast Guard refurbished the lower half of the lighthouse while the Project Bug group raised funds to restore the interior and upper parts. Solar power replaced the battery system.

However, the Project Bug Light dissolved after a few years, the five-year lease expired and plans were again made to replace the lighthouse. A new preservation effort was undertaken and the Coast Guard again refurbished the lighthouse in 1996; fund raising for maintenance is ongoing. Although the light can be seen distantly from the Plymouth waterfront, best views are from the harbor cruises or whale watches out of Plymouth.

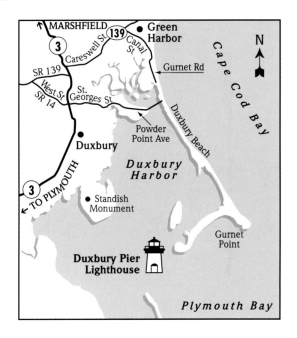

**Directions:**
From the intersection of RTs 14 and 139, bear right (east) and continue on RT 14 (West St.). Cross MA 3 and continue straight as the road becomes St. Georges St. Follow this road to Powder Point Ave. which ends at a bridge to the Gurnet peninsula and beach parking area. The light may be seen from Duxbury Beach and the Gurnet peninsula; a four-wheel drive vehicle is required to drive past the parking areas onto the Gurnet. Additionally, the light may be viewed at a distance from Plymouth Harbor or more closely from excursion boats from the Plymouth Municipal Pier.

# Minots Ledge Light

In 1847, lighthouse inspector I.W.P. Lewis compiled a report on dangerous Minots Ledge off Boston's south shore. The report noted that more than 40 vessels had been lost on the ledge from 1832 to 1841, with property damage in excess of $360,000. Lewis stated that need for a lighthouse at Minots Ledge was greater than anywhere else in New England.

This recommendation led to construction of the first lighthouse at the ledge built between 1847 and 1850, lighted for the first time January 1, 1850. Minots was the first lighthouse in the United States to be exposed to the ocean's full fury and the first two keepers deemed the structure unsafe. These fears proved well founded. In April of 1851 a storm struck the New England coast, flooding Boston and much of the area. People on shore the night of April 16 heard the fog bell at the lighthouse, then sudden silence. Two assistant keepers were killed and legend tells that, in dark and stormy weather, a voice can be heard coming from Minots light warning, "Stay Away!"

From 1851 to 1860 a lightship replaced the tower and work on a new stone tower was undertaken in 1855. This structure has been called the greatest achievement in American lighthouse engineering. Because construction could take place only at low tide on calm days, the cutting and assembling of the granite took place on Government Island. A total of 1,079 blocks of Quincy granite were placed.

*"So it may stand, that 'they who go down to the sea in ships' may see this signal fire burning brightly to warn them from the countless rocks that echo with the rage that oft swells from the bosom of old ocean."*

Cap't. Barton Alexander,
Superintendant of Minots Light construction

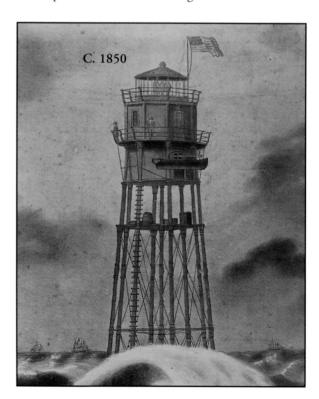

C. 1850

Many times during the construction waves swept workers off the rocks but the project continued and the last stone was placed at Minots Ledge on June 29, 1860. The lantern room and second-order Fresnel lens were installed and the lighthouse illuminated on August 22, 1860. Although waves have been known to sweep over the top of the lighthouse, the structure has withstood countless storms and hurricanes, a testament to the designers and builders.

A well in the lower part of the tower, filled twice yearly, held the water supply for the keepers. A member of a group of young ladies touring the lighthouse asked the keeper about the well. He answered,"That's our bathtub. It goes down 40 feet." Mulling this over, the lady replied, " You must be out of luck when you drop the soap." In 1893 Minots was given a new optic and a distinctive characteristic 1-4-3 flash. Someone allowed that 1-4-3 stood for "I Love You", giving rise to the nickname the "I Love You Light".

The lighthouse was automated in 1947 and the Fresnel lens replaced; in 1983 the light was converted to solar power. In 1992-93 the keeper's house at Government Island was restored with funds raised by the Cohasset Lightkeepers Corporation. At Government Island, a replica of the lantern room of Minots light sits atop some of the granite blocks removed from the lighthouse during a renovation in 1989; the fog bell also is on display.

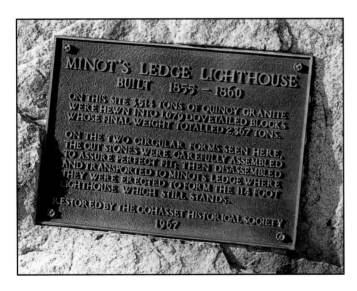

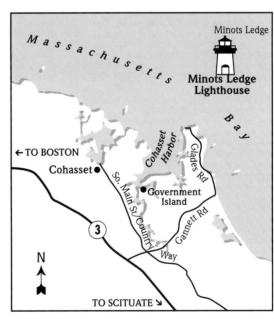

**Directions:** Land views of the lighthouse are distant from Sandy Beach in Cohasset. From Cohasset center, turn east on Highland Ave then east onto Beach St. Continue to Atlantic Ave. and turn left; the beach is about 0.5 mile north. Minots is best photographed from the water; excursion boats out of Boston Harbor which specifically offer "lighthouse trips" (Friends of Boston Harbor Is. or Harbor Explorers) usually try to get to this lighthouse. However, sea conditions are often unpredictable in the area making close views of the light impossible.

# Scituate Light

By the late 18th century Scituate had become a major fishing port, due in large part to its protected harbor. However, shallow water and mudflats made entering the harbor difficult and, in 1810, pressure from town officials convinced the federal government to appropriate $4000 for construction of a lighthouse at the harbor entrance. Completed in 1811, the 25-foot stone tower exhibited a white light 30 feet above sea level and was accompanied by a keeper's house, oil vault and well.

The first keeper of Scituate Light was Simeon Bates who remained at the lighthouse until his death in 1834. Bates and his wife, Rachel, had nine children, including teenage daughters Rebecca and Abigail. During the War of 1812, British warships frequently raided New England coastal towns, including Scituate. In September 1814, such a raid was attempted as a warship anchored close to the Scituate lighthouse.

The only members of the Bates family at the station were Rebecca and Abigail. The sisters, seeing a party of British soldiers rowing toward shore, realized there wasn't time to warn others. They grabbed their fife and drum and played loudly; the unsuspecting British thought the Scituate town militia was approaching and hastily retreated. Thus was created the legend of Scituate's "Lighthouse Army of Two." Some have claimed the ghosts of Rebecca and Abigail Bates haunt Scituate Light. Fife and drum music, they say, can be heard blending in with wind and waves.

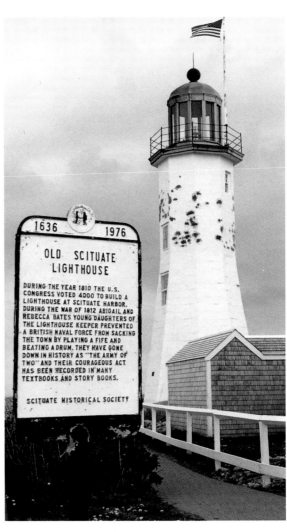

In 1827 a 15-foot brick extension and new lantern room were added to the lighthouse to increase its visibility. A white-over-red configuration (white top light, red light in lower windows) was intended to allow mariners to differentiate between Scituate and Boston lights. However, the white and red lights tended to merge from a distance and vessels continued to crash into the dangerous offshore ledges. The lighthouse gradually deteriorated and the completion of Minots Light in 1850 signalled the end for Scituate light. When the first Minots light was destroyed in a storm in 1852, Scituate light went back into service and it received a new Fresnel lens in 1855. In 1860 the second Minots was lighted and Scituate extinguished. In 1916 the U.S. Lighthouse Establishment put Scituate Light up for sale. A hastily organized deposit of $1000 secured the property for the Town of Scituate. Among those who later contributed to the $4000 purchase price was a grand nephew of Abigail and Rebecca Bates.

The town made some initial improvements and did major work on the keeper's house in the 1960s. In 1988 the light was placed on the National Register of Historic Places and in 1994 was relighted as a private aid to navigation. Today contributions and rent from residents of the keeper's house pay for upkeep of the property.

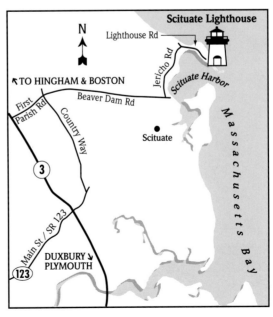

**Directions:**
From MA 3, take the MA 123 exit east to MA 3A .Bear left onto Country Way and continue to the intersection with First Parish Rd. Or, coming from the north on MA 3A, turn left onto First Parish Rd. **Both** MA 3A and Country Way intersect with First Parish Rd. Bear right onto Beaver Dam Rd. (First Parish bears left), continue to the intersection with Jericho Rd. and turn left. Continue to Lighthouse Rd.; bear right to the lighthouse. There is a parking area.

# Plymouth Light

The area around Plymouth and the Gurnet was visited and mapped by explorer Samuel de Champlain in 1606. The name apparently referred to similar areas in England which were named after the abundant fish called gurnet. Plymouth became a major port of colonial America and shipping traffic necessitated a navigational aid at the entrance to the harbor. In 1769 the first lighthouse was erected on the high bluff at the end of the long Gurnet peninsula; the house, with two lantern rooms on the roof, was the first site of "twin lights" in North America.

The original lighthouse was built on the land of John and Hannah Thomas; he would serve as the first keeper and, after his death, she became America's first woman lightkeeper. This twin structure served until 1801 when it was destroyed by an oil fire; new twin towers were built in 1803, 30 feet apart. However, there were complaints that the Gurnet's two lights blended into one from a distance and were easily confused with Barnstable's Sandy Neck Light. In 1843 the towers were replaced with octagonal wooden structures, 34 feet high and connected with a covered walkway. The problem of "merging lights" remained and in 1871 the power of the lights was increased by installation of fourth-order Fresnel lenses.

Gurnet Light, Plymouth, Mass.

Gurnet Lights and Keeper's Residence, Plymouth, Mass.

The importance of Plymouth light gradually decreased as commerce declined. In 1924 the northeast light was discontinued but that foundation is still visible next to the remaining structure. The light was automated in 1986 and converted to solar power in 1994; a modern optic replaced the Fresnel lens. The Massachusetts chapter of the U.S. Lighthouse Society was granted lease to the lighthouse in the late 1980s but the lease has since reverted to the Coast Guard. The lighthouse was moved back from the eroding cliff in 1997.

**Directions:** From RT 3, take the RT 14/Duxbury exit east. Bear left at the intersection with MA 139 (Careswell St.) and continue to Canal St. Turning right follow Canal St.; the road becomes Gurnet Rd. and ends at parking areas for Duxbury Beach. A four-wheel drive vehicle is required for the remainder of the drive along the sandy peninsula to its end at the lighthouse. A permit also may be needed.

**Or..** From the intersection of RTs 14 and 139, bear right and continue on RT 14 (West St.). Cross MA 3 and continue straight as the road becomes St. Georges St. Follow this road to Powder Point Ave. which ends at a bridge to the Gurnet peninsula and beach parking area.

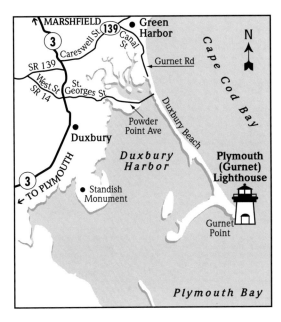

55

# The Southeastern Shore

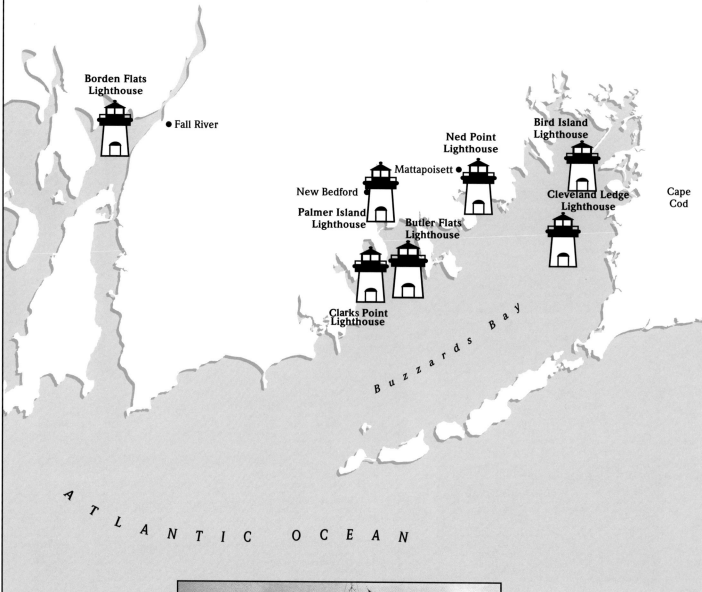

Borden Flats
Lighthouse

● Fall River

New Bedford ●

Palmer Island
Lighthouse

Butler Flats
Lighthouse

Clarks Point
Lighthouse

Mattapoisett ●

Ned Point
Lighthouse

Bird Island
Lighthouse

Cleveland Ledge
Lighthouse

Cape
Cod

Buzzards Bay

ATLANTIC OCEAN

# Borden Flats Light

The city of Fall River is famous as the home town of Lizzie Borden, who was acquitted of the ax murder of her father and stepmother. Borden Flats Light was named for Lizzie's family, one of the most prominent in Fall River, years before the murders.

Built in 1881 near the Braga Bridge crossing the Taunton River, Borden Flats light is built entirely of cast iron plates on a concrete caisson base. The lighthouse received a fourth-order Fresnel lens. After being battered in the Hurricane of 1938 (as were most lighthouses on New England's south-facing coast), a new, wider cylindrical caisson was built around the old one. A cistern is on the first level, with five stories above, two of which were used as living quarters.

Borden Flats light was automated in 1963 and in 1977 its Fresnel lens was replaced by a modern plastic lens. The lighthouse can be seen easily from the bridge and shore points in Fall River.

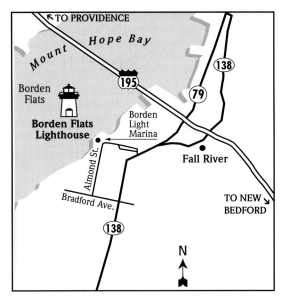

**Directions:**
From I-195 or Rt 24 take MA 138 South (Broadway) into Fall River. Turn west onto Bradford St. then right onto Almond St. Follow Almond St. to the dead end at Park Street and turn into the Borden Light Marina; the lighthouse is to the west of the marina.

# Palmer Island Light

New Bedford was the whaling capital of the nation in the mid-nineteenth century and in 1849 a lighthouse was built on the northern point of Palmer Island on the west side of the entrance to the harbor. The 24-foot tower was built of rubblestone with wooden windows and floors.In the 1860s a hotel and dance hall were built on the southern side of Palmer Island. The hotel was a favorite stop for returning whalers; not surprisingly illegal activity also flourished. An amusement park was built in 1890 but it soon failed and the hotel burned in 1905.

The island has been the scene of great heroism and tragedy, in particular the tale of keeper Arthur Small. On September 21, 1938, the worst hurricane in New England history battered the south-facing coast. That afternoon Small left for the lighthouse, a 350-foot walk from the keeper's house and was struck by a sudden tidal wave. He looked back to see his wife attempting to launch a rowboat to reach him. Small somehow made it back to the tower to tend the light; Mabel Small did not survive.

The lighthouse was automated in 1941 but with the construction of a massive hurricane wall in New Bedford harbor in the 1960s, the light was deemed unnecessary. In 1966 the tower was burned by arsonists; renovations in 1989 were soon lost to futher vandalism. Until recently Palmer Island was littered with debris, the lighthouse an empty shell and the lantern room empty. A local group has now accomplished restoration and improvement of the site. The lighthouse is featured on the city seal of New Bedford with the motto "I Spread the Light." The light is accessible at low tide from the hurricane wall. (**Note directions and map, next page**)

58

# Clark's Point Light

A 42-foot stone tower, built in 1804, was the first lighthouse at Clark's Point to guide vessels into New Bedford Harbor. In the 1860s a seven-sided granite fort was built next to the light. Because the walls of Fort Taber eventually blocked the view of the light, in 1869 the lantern room and keeper's quarters were relocated to the top of the fort. The old stone light tower stood until it was demolished in 1906.

In 1889 a new lighthouse (Butler Flats Light) was built offshore from Clark's Point. The light at Clark's Point was then discontinued but the stone tower not demolished until 1906. Listed in the National Register of Historic Places, the fort and lighthouse were restored in the 1970s only to fall victim to extensive vandalism and theft. After years of neglect and decay, the lighthouse was recently restored by The City of New Bedford and relit on June 15, 2001, the 132nd anniversary of the lighting of the beacon.

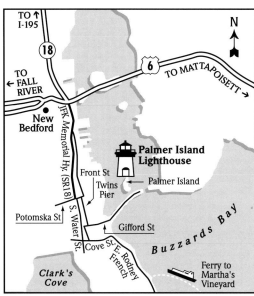

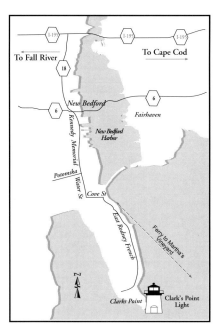

**Directions:**

**PALMER ISLAND**: From I-195 in New Bedford, take the MA 18 (Downtown) exit south. Continue on MA 18 south to Cove St. and turn left;follow Cove St. to its end at the hurricane wall and bear right. Park along a side street or in marked lots and walk up along the wall back north. A paved path continues to the right and leads to the island which can be accessed at low tide. **Alternatively..** turn left onto Potomska St. from MA 18, then right onto Front St. At Gifford St. turn left and continue to a parking lot behind industrial buildings.

**CLARK'S POINT:** From I-95 in New Bedford, take the MA 18 (Downtown) exit south. Continue on MA 18 (Kennedy Memorial Highway/Water St) to Cove St. Turn left onto East Rodey French Blvd. Continue to the park, Fort Taber and the lighthouse.

# Butler Flats Light

Built in shallow water without solid rock for foundation, Butler Flats light was a challenge to construct in 1898 to replace Clark's Point Light. An iron cylinder 35 feet in diameter was placed then filled with stone and concrete; the brick lighthouse was built on top. The sparkplug-style light, similar in appearance to Boston's Deer Island Light, has four stories and originally had a fifth-order Fresnel lens. Butler Flats had only three keepers from its first lighting until 1942 when the Coast Guard took over from the Lighthouse Service.

In 1975 a new automatic light and fog signal were placed on New Bedford's hurricane barrier and the lighthouse was deemed unnecessary. It was automated and became one of the first solar-powered lighthouses. After decommissioning in 1978 the light came under control of the City of New Bedford and a private group took responsibility for maintenance of the light. Best views of Butler Flats are from the New Bedford-Martha's Vineyard ferry.

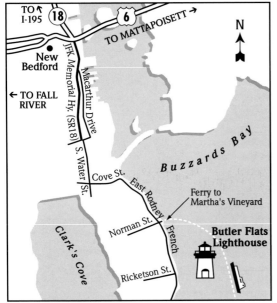

**Directions**: From I-195 or US RT 6 in New Bedford, take MA 18 south; continue on MA 18/Water St. to Cove Rd. Turn left (east) onto Cove Rd. Bear right at the intersection with East Rodney French, passing the New Bedford ferry terminal. Continue to the intersection with Ricketson St; the seawall just south of Ricketson St. affords best views. Parking is restricted along East Rodney French, but not along the side streets. There are free parking lots closeby. The light is best photographed from the ferry to Martha's Vineyard.

**New Bedford Ferry:** Turn left off East Rodney French at Norman St. The ferry runs daily late May through Columbus Day; crossing time is about 90 minutes. Cape Island Express Lines, Inc., P.O. Box J-405, New Bedford, MA 02741 (508) 997-1688.

# Cleveland Ledge Light

At the western entrance to the Cape Cod Canal, Cleveland Ledge Light is the last commissioned lighthouse built in New England and the only one built by the Coast Guard. The project was started by the state of Massachusetts in 1940 then transferred to the federal government in 1941 and finished in 1943. Cleveland Ledge was named for President Grover Cleveland who frequently fished in the area. The style of this lighthouse is unique among New England lighthouses, having been described as "uncharacteristic of any frugal, Yankee heritage." A 50-foot tower sits atop two stories that were used as living and work quarters; the entire structure sits on a 52-foot cylindrical caisson pier.

On September 14, 1944 a hurricane battered the lighthouse, dislodging a glass block skylight and allowing water to wash through the structure. The nine-man crew had to bail water from the engine room as the water level neared the batteries which powered the station. Fortunately the water stopped rising about two inches below the batteries, allowing the light to continue flashing throughout the storm.

The lighthouse originally had a fourth-order Fresnel lens. In 1978 the lens was replaced, the light automated and the lighthouse sealed off. The Coast Guard completed renovations in 1990. The light must be photographed from the water.

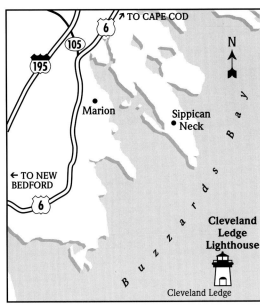

## Ned Point Light

The first lighthouse at Ned Point, at the northeast side of the entrance to Mattapoisett Harbor on Buzzard's Bay, was a 35-foot rubblestone tower built in 1837 at a cost of $4500. The construction was not yet complete when an inspector arrived, so the contractor took him to the nearby tavern he owned while workers attempted to make the structure appear finished. The ruse failed however, when the inspector stepped on loose planking, falling into the foundation of the tower.

A new 39-foot tower was built in 1888 and a fifth-order Fresnel lens added. The keeper's house was removed in 1930 and floated by barge across Buzzard's Bay to Wing's Neck Light in Bourne. Legend has it that the last keeper made the trip in the house, cooking breakfast along the way across the bay.

The Coast Guard decommissioned Ned Point light in 1952; the site surrounding the tower was sold to the Town of Mattapoisett in 1958 and developed into a park. The light was reactivated in 1961.

Ned point is a popular spot for weddings and engagements, with the lighthouse as backdrop. The Coast Guard repainted and refurbished the tower in 1995, installing a new optic as well. The area and lighthouse are well-tended and easily accessible all year.

Ned Point Light, Mattapoisett, Mass.

C. 1909

**Directions:**
**From I-195** (north): Take the Mattapoisett exit and follow North Street into town. Turn east (left) onto Water St; continue on Water St./Beacon St. to Ned Point Rd. and bear right. Follow Ned Point Rd. for about 0.5 mile to Ned Point and the light. **From US Rt 6** (from Cape Cod or New Bedford): Continue into Mattapoisett and turn east onto Water St. Follow Water St./Beacon St. to Ned Point Rd. and bear right. Follow Ned Point Rd. for about 0.5 mile to Ned Point and the light. There is a park with picnic tables and parking area at the lighthouse.

# Bird Island Light

Located in Sippican Harbor, near the town of Marion, the first Bird Island light was built in 1819. The 25-foot rubblestone tower was one of the first lighthouses of that time to receive a revolving optic. Local legend says that the first keeper, William Moore, was a pirate, banished to Bird Island as punishment. However, others note that his letters during that time mention a boat and his work on various inventions, casting doubt that Mr. Moore was a pirate-prisoner. Some accounts further claim that Moore murdered his wife at the lighthouse and disappeared soon thereafter. A gun reportedly was found in a secret hiding place when the original keeper's house was razed; some believe it was the murder weapon. Keeper Moore denied the charges, claiming the effects of tobacco caused his wife's death. Although she is supposedly buried on the island, there is no sign of the grave.

In 1889 the rubblestone tower was refurbished and equipped with a flashing fourth-order Fresnel lens; a new keeper's house was subsequently added. The last keeper at Bird Island (1919-1926) was Maurice Babcock who later became the last civilian keeper at Boston Light. The lighthouse was taken out of service in June 1935 as ship traffic in the area had diminished greatly. Every building on Bird Island except the lighthouse tower was destroyed by the Hurrican of '38; some local residents claim to have seen the stations fog bell being swept off the island in the storm.

In 1939 the island was sold to private ownership and since 1966 the property has been owned by the town of Marion. The Town of Marion and Sippican Historical Society raised $13,000 for repairs to the lighthouse and on July 9, 1976 Bird Island light was relighted as a private aid to navigation. Vandals damaged the optic in 1981 rendering the light nonfunctional. In 1994 a new effort to restore the light was mounted by the Bird Island Preservation Society. Private funds and federal grants enabled restoration of the lighthouse tower and Bird Island Light was relit as a private aid to navigation on July 4, 1997; the optic is solar powered.

The island is now considered an important nesting site for common terns and endangered roseate terns. Although visible distantly from shore, the light is best viewed by boat.

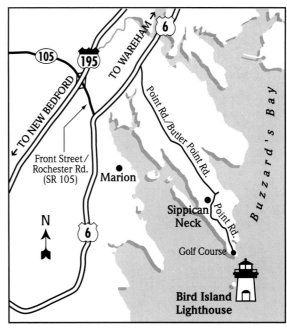

**Directions:**
**From I-195:** Take the MA 105 exit south (becomes Front/Rochester St.); continue to US Rt 6 and turn north (left). Go about 1.5 miles to Butler Point/Point Rd and turn south. Continue on this road across Sippican Neck to the road's end at a golf course. The lighthouse can be seen in the distance from along the seawall.
**From US 6:** From Marion, continue north about 1.5 miles past the intersection with MA 105 (Front/Rochester St.). Turn south onto Butler Point/Point Rd. and follow the road to it's end at the golf course.From Wareham, continue south to to "MarionTown Limit" sign and go approximately 0.5 mile to the intersection of Rt 6 and Butler Point/Point Rd. Turn south onto Butler Point/ Point Rd. and follow the road to it's end at the golf course.

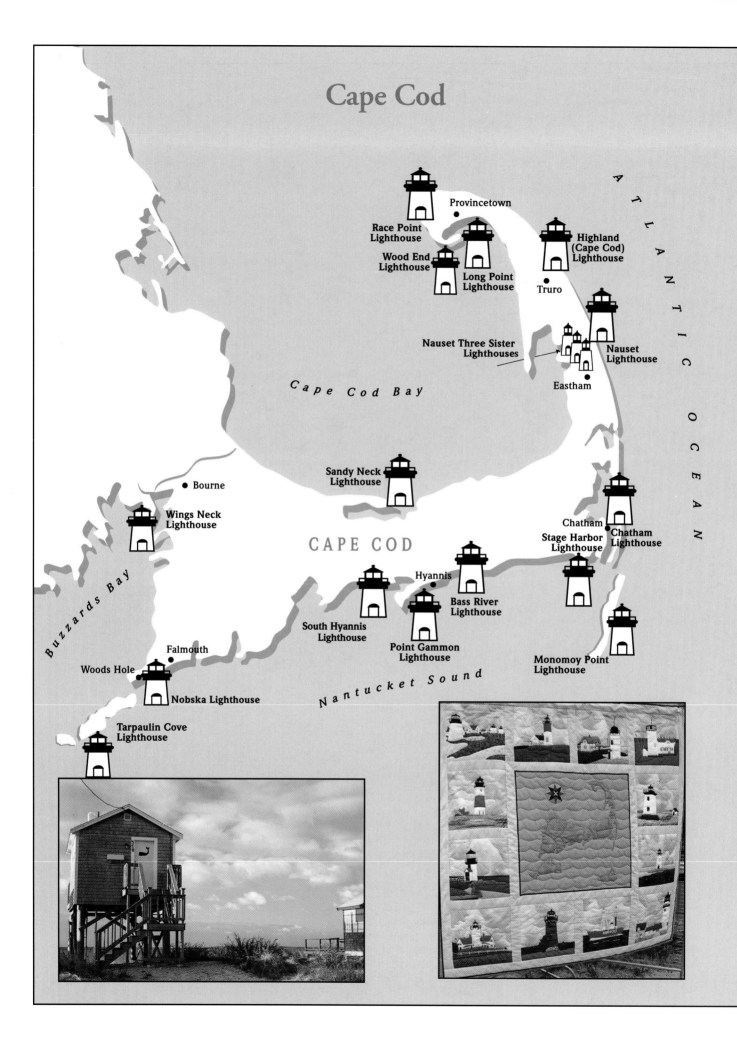

# Cape Cod

Race Point
Lighthouse

Provincetown

Wood End
Lighthouse

Long Point
Lighthouse

Highland
(Cape Cod)
Lighthouse

Truro

Nauset Three Sister
Lighthouses

Nauset
Lighthouse

Eastham

*Cape Cod Bay*

Sandy Neck
Lighthouse

Bourne

CAPE COD

Wings Neck
Lighthouse

Hyannis

Chatham

Stage Harbor
Lighthouse

Chatham
Lighthouse

Bass River
Lighthouse

South Hyannis
Lighthouse

Point Gammon
Lighthouse

Monomoy Point
Lighthouse

*Buzzards Bay*

Falmouth

Woods Hole

Nobska Lighthouse

*Nantucket Sound*

Tarpaulin Cove
Lighthouse

*A T L A N T I C   O C E A N*

# Wings Neck Light

The peninsula called Wings Neck extends from Pocasset on Cape Cod into Buzzard's Bay, a busy thorofare in the 19th century. The first Wings Neck Light, built in 1848, was a Cape-Cod style structure, with a wooden lantern room atop a stone keeper's house. A Fresnel lens was added in 1856. Although a fire badly damaged the structure in 1878, a new keeper's house and attached octagonal lighthouse were not completed until 1890.

President Warren Harding, in the presidental yacht *Mayflower,* frequently passed near the station and anchored nearby in foul weather. The keeper took note of the anchored yacht and gave the President a 21-gun salute on the station's fog bell.

In 1930 the keeper's house at Ned Point Light in Mattapoisett was floated across Cape Cod to become an assistant keeper's dwelling at Wings Neck. Not long after, however, with the building of Cleveland Ledge Light, Wings Neck Light was considered expendable. The station was discontinued in 1945 and sold in 1947. The new owners were a musical family and the property became a center of musical activity, including visits from the Trapp family singers. The lighthouse is on private property; the grounds are not accessible to the public.

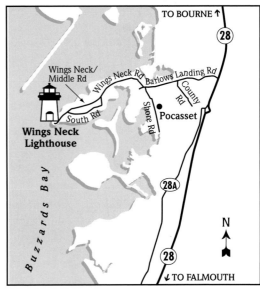

**Directions**: Follow US RT 6 to the Bourne rotary and bear south onto MA 28
heading to Falmouth. At the Wing's Neck/Pocasset sign turn right (west) onto Barlow's Landing Rd. Continue west, crossing County and Shore Roads;  bear right onto Wing's Neck Rd. The road divides but either route will take you to a cul-de-sac.  The lighthouse may be viewed from the cul-de-sac; there are parking and trespassing restrictions. Cleveland East Ledge light is seen in the distance to the southwest offshore.

# Tarpaulin Cove Light

Naushon Island is the largest of the Elizabeth Islands, which extend into Buzzard's Bay in a line from Falmouth on Cape Cod. A beacon was placed on the island by a tavern keeper in 1759 for the "public good of whalemen and coasters". The light was maintained by tavern keepers for 58 years then sold to the federal government in 1817.

In 1817 a 38-foot rubblestone lighthouse tower was built and a Fresnel lens installed in 1856. The tower may also have been rebuilt at that time. The old stone keeper's house was replaced in 1888 and in 1891 a new 28-foot brick lighthouse was built. A fog bell in a tower also was installed; the bell tower was destroyed in the hurricane of 1938.

The light was automated in 1941, after which the house and other buildings fell into disrepair and were torn down in 1962. The Fresnel lens was replaced as well. The island is privately owned and the lighthouse difficult to view except by private boat.

*Tarpaulin Cove lighthouse "keepers"*

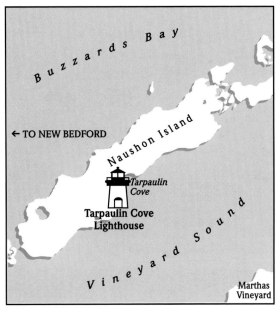

### Directions:

The lighthouse is located on Naushon Island off Woods Hole and
Martha's Vineyard.  It may only be viewed by private boat; the island is privately owned, accessible to residents only.

# Sandy Neck Light

Barnstable was a thriving fishing port and shipyard in the early 19th century. Sandy Neck light was built in 1827 at the west side of the entrance to the harbor, at the tip of the barrier dunes. The first lighthouse was a typical Cape Cod style structure, with a wooden lantern on the roof of a brick keeper's house. In 1857 this lighthouse was replaced by the brick one that still stands; a new Victorian-style keeper's house was built in 1880. In 1887 the cracked brick tower was strengthened with two iron hoops and six staves. This addition is still in place, giving the tower a "distinctive" look.

Because Barnstable harbor was frequently icebound in winter, many crews from trapped vessels were brought to the light station. However the harbor, virtually inaccessible from January to March, gradually declined in importance and shifting sands left the lighthouse in a less advantageous position. In 1931 the light was decommissioned and the lens moved to a skeleton tower closer to the tip of Sandy Neck. This tower was discontinued in 1952, the lantern room and lens removed and the entire property sold to private ownership.

Sandy Neck light can be seen in the distance from Millway Beach in Barnstable or by boat. Public access to the property is not permitted as it is on the Sandy Neck Wildlife Refuge. Four-wheel drive, permits, and vehicle inspection are required prior to entering the area

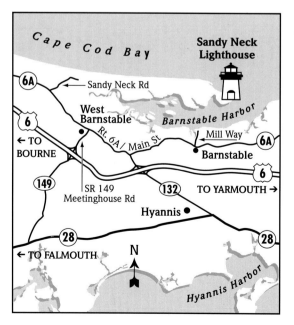

C. 1912

**Directions:** From US Rt 6 take the MA 149 exit and turn north to Barnstable & West Barnstable. Turn left onto MA 6A (Main Street) and continue to Mill Way. Turn north and continue across a bridge to the dock and beach area. The lighthouse can be seen in the distance across Barnstable Harbor. The lighthouse is most easily photographed by boat. The Sandy Neck area in West Barnstable is a wildlife refuge. There is no public access to the light; permits and four-wheel drive vehicle are required and limited entrance strictly enforced.

# Nobska Point Light

Located between Buzzard's Bay and Vineyard Sound, Nobska Point light stands out on the rocky headlands above Woods Hole Harbor. The first lighthouse at Nobska Point was built in 1828, a typical Cape Cod structure with the octagonal lantern room on top of the keeper's house. In 1876 the light was rebuilt as a 40-foot cast-iron tower lined with brick; a fifth-order Fresnel lens was installed and the new tower painted red. This lighthouse is one of only three lighthouses with miniature brass light-houses as ornamentation atop each balustrade on the gallery (Cape Neddick and Lubec Channel, both in Maine, are the others). Nobska was upgraded to a fourth-order Fresnel lens in 1888; that lens remains in place.

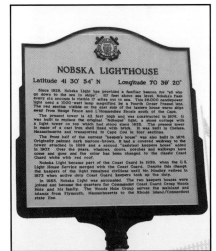

*(Continued, following pages)*

71

NOBSKA LIGHTHOUSE

1828                                            1876

LAT 41 30' 54" N          LONG 70 39' 20" w
Present tower built 1876
Original NOBSQUE LIGHT 1828
87' above sea level          Visible 17 miles out to sea
Nobska Light has been placed on the National Register of Historic Places

Presented by the Falmouth Historical Commission

## Nobska Point Light

The light was automated in 1985 and now serves as the home for the Group Commander of the Woods Hole Coast Guard Base. The lighthouse is easily accessible with a small parking area adjacent; grounds are open to the public. Ferries from Woods Hole to Martha's Vineyard also pass Nobska Point.

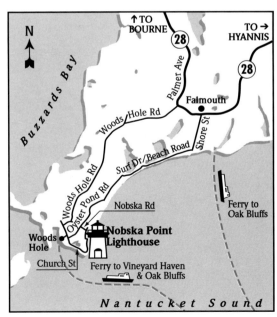

### Directions:

Take MA 28 (from the north or east) into Falmouth. Coming from the east: turn south at the intersection of Main St. (MA 28) and Shore St.
Follow Shore St./ Surf Dr./Beach Rd. along the shore.; bear left at the intersection with Nobska Rd. and continue to the lighthouse.
**Or...**if coming into Falmouth on MA 28 from the north, bear right (west) off MA 28 (Palmer St.) to Woods Hole Rd. Follow the road toward Woods Hole (signs direct you easily). Turn left onto Church St. and follow the road to the lighthouse. Continuing around past the lighthouse, Nobska Rd. joins Oyster Pond Rd.; you've made a loop which leads back to Falmouth. "Vineyard Boat" & "Woods Hole" signs begin well outside Falmouth from all directions and clearly indicate the way.

# South Hyannis Light

In the mid 1800s Hyannis Harbor was a busy fishing and trade port and a harbor light was needed to guide mariners into the busy area. The first light was a privately-built shack on the beach, with a lamp hung in a window. Congress then authorized construction of a lighthouse at South Hyannis in 1848 and a small tower was built. A larger lantern room was installed in 1856 to accommodate a Fresnel lens. In 1885 a lamp hoisted atop a 20-foot tower was added on a nearby wharf to serve as a range light. South Hyannis Light was discontinued in 1929 and the entire lantern room removed.

The lighthouse and keeper's dwelling were sold at auction and subsequently passed through various ownership. Current owners have completed extensive restoration of the property but added an unconventional lantern room, now used as a sitting area. Although the light is slightly visible from the street, best views are from excursion boats in the harbor area.

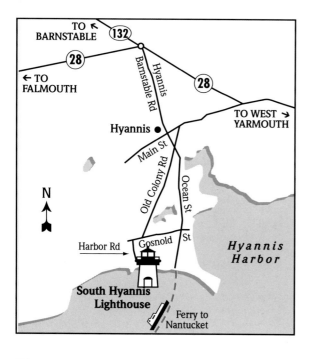

**Directions:**
At the intersection of MA 132 and MA 28, turn south onto Hyannis/Barnstable Rd(to Hyannis Center). Follow signs to the Nantucket Ferry Ocean St. Dock. Turn south onto Ocean St. and continue to Gosnold St. Turn right, pass Old Colony Rd to the right and continue to Harbor Rd. Turn left, following Harbor Rd. The lighthouse is to your right at the end of the road.

# Point Gammon Light

Point Gammon on Great Island is just to the east of the entrance to Hyannis Harbor and about 2.5 miles from the dangerous ledges known as Bishops and Clerks. The fieldstone lighthouse was erected in 1816 in a style unique to New England lighthouses, its stonework and narrow windows suggesting a castle in the British Isles. In 1855 keeper John Peak counted 4,969 schooners, 1,455 sloops, 216 brigs and four steamboats passing his station. Point Gammon light was considered inadequate for this level of traffic, prompting the location of a lightship close to the Bishops and Clerks ledges. In 1858 the lightship was replaced by the Bishops and Clerks lighthouse (now defunct).

Great Island was subsequently sold to private ownership; in 1935 the old stone house was dismantled and the stones used to build a new dwelling on the island. The tower was converted into a summer residence in 1970, with the lantern room refitted as a bedroom; the structure is now empty however. All of the 600-acre Great Island is now private property with no public access. The lighthouse can be viewed distantly from the Hyannis-Nantucket ferry or from fishing and excursion boats leaving Hyannis.

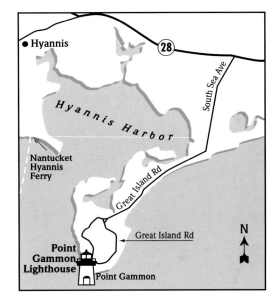

**Directions:**
The island is privately owned and access is closely restricted; there is no public entrance to the lighthouse. Distant views also are possible from the Hyannis-Nantucket ferries and from the Hyannis to Nantucket flights.

75

# Monomoy Point Light

Extending southward from Chatham at the elbow of Cape Cod's curling arm, Monomoy is at present two islands but was at one time a peninsula connected to the mainland. The area was long a graveyard for vessels due to unusually strong tidal currents. These treacherous currents prompted the Pilgrims to enter Cape Cod Bay, settling at Plymouth rather than continuing on to Virginia.

In the early 19th century a settlement grew up at Monomoy and increased traffic in the area from the fishing industry made a lighthouse necessary. Cape Cod's fifth lighthouse was built at Monomoy Point in 1823, eight miles from Chatham near the southern end of the peninsula. The first lighthouse was a lantern room on the roof of the keeper's house. It appears the lighthouse was rebuilt twice, with the present cast-iron, brick-lined tower built somewhere between 1855 and 1872; two lifesaving stations also were built in 1872. To make it more visible by day, the tower was painted red in 1882.

With the 1914 opening of the Cape Cod Canal, and the increased power of Chatham light, Monomoy light was considered expendable. The light was discontinued in 1923 and the property sold to private ownership. In 1964 the Massachusetts Audubon Society restored the lighthouse and keeper's house; a federal grant funded further refurbishing in 1988.

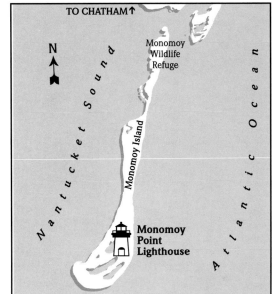

TO CHATHAM ↑

N

Nantucket Sound

Monomoy
Wildlife
Refuge

Monomoy Island

Atlantic Ocean

Monomoy
Point
Lighthouse

The Blizzard of 1978 cut Monomoy into two islands--North and South Monomoy--both of which are managed currently by the U.S. Fish and Wildlife Service. The Cape Cod Museum of Natural History offers day trips to the island and overnight stays in the keeper's house.

**Directions:** The islands of North and South Monomoy are nine miles south of Chatham; the lighthouse is on the south island. Bird watching trips are offered by the Audubon Society out of Wellfleet ; the Cape Cod Musuem of Natural History also offers trips with overnights possible  P.O. Box 1710, Brewster, MA. 1-800-479-3867

# Stage Harbor Light

This lighthouse is one of the most recent of the Cape Cod lighthouses. Because the area was busy with fishing traffic and thick fog common, the Lighthouse Board recommended in 1876 that a lighthouse be built on Hardings Beach on the northeast side of the channel known as Chatham Roads. A 48-foot iron tower and wooden keeper's house were completed in 1880 at a cost of $10,000; a fifth-order Fresnel lens was installed.

For a time during prohibition, the floor under the covered walkway between the house and tower became a hiding place for liquor. An inspector on a surprise visit noticed the loose floorboards, but much to the keeper's relief merely advised him to nail them down better. In 1933 an automated light on a skeleton tower replaced Stage Harbor Light. The lantern was removed and the tower capped.

The property is now privately owned. There has never been electricity at the site and no plumbing save a single pump. The lighthouse may be viewed distantly from the harbor; a one-mile walk over sand from Hardings Beach parking area ends at the light.

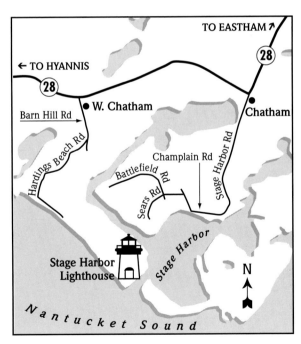

**Directions:**
From MA 28 in Chatham/West Chatham, turn south onto Barn Hill Rd. Bear right onto Hardings Beach Rd. and continue to its end at the beach parking area. The lighthouse is about a mile east from the beach along a footpath across the sand dunes.

Alternatively, the lighthouse may be viewed from across Stage Harbor. At the Chatham rotary on MA 28, turn south onto Stage Harbor Rd. and continue south onto Champlain Rd. for about 1.5 miles. Bear left at the intersection of Champlain Rd. and Battlefield Rd. into Sears Rd. Turn left onto Sears Point Rd. and continue for approximately 0.5mile to the road's end at a public boat landing.

# Bass River Light

The Bass River Lighthouse, now the Lighthouse Inn, barely resembles the original structure built in 1855; only the lantern room on the roof remains visible amid the additions. In 1850 Congress appropriated $4,000 for a lighthouse in West Dennis to guide vessels through Nantucket Sound. Until this time a man named William Crowell kept a lantern burning in his attic window to aid local mariners; ship captains paid for his lantern oil by donating 25 cents a month. When the lighthouse was completed Crowell appropriately became the first keeper and remained in the position until 1880 save for a nine-year stint in the Union army during the Civil War.

Bass River light was discontinued in 1880 and sold at auction after the lighting of Stage Harbor light in Chatham. Six months later complaints caused the government to buy the lighthouse back, relighting it in 1881. However, with the advent of the Cape Cod Canal and installation of an automated beacon at the entrance to Bass River, the lighthouse was considered unnecessary. The light was extinguished in 1914 and its fourth-order Fresnel lens removed.

The property passed into private ownership and was opened as the Lighthouse Inn in 1938. In 1989 the light was reactivated as a private aid to navigation with a 300mm optic providing assistance to local mariners.

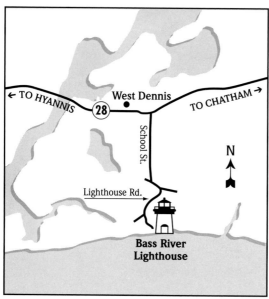

**Directions:** On MA 28 in West Dennis, turn south onto School St. (just east of the Bass River Bridge). Continue to Lighthouse Road and turn right; it is about 0.5 mile to the Lighthouse Inn Road. Turn left and continue to the parking lot at the inn. There is a paved path on the east side of the inn that leads to a seawall.

# Chatham Light

Established in 1808, Chatham light station was intended to give Cape Cod a second lighthouse to assist mariners making the difficult trip from Nantucket Sound around the Cape. The obvious choice for this light was Chatham, at the elbow of Cape Cod's crooked "arm".

To distinguish Chatham from Highland Light, it was decided to make Chatham a twin light station. The first octagonal twin towers were built of wood, each one 40 feet high, about 70 feet apart. A small one-bedroom dwelling also was built; Samuel Nye was appointed first keeper by President Thomas Jefferson. The twin lights had six lamps each, with 8.5 inch parabolic reflectors and green glass lenses. This system, the Argand lamp, was devised by Winslow Lewis. Although an efficient system, the reflective coating quickly wore off with repeated polishings and the green lenses diminished the lights' brightness. Nevertheless Winslow's system was used for several decades in American lighthouses.

The first Chatham twin lights lasted 33 years, then were replaced by 40-foot brick towers, built further from the rapidly eroding cliff. In 1857 both lights received fourth-order Fresnel lenses, each showing a fixed white light.

By 1877, erosion from storms had "relocated" the Chatham lights from 228 feet to only 48 feet from the edge of a 50-foot cliff. In December 1879 the south tower fell to the beach below; 15 months later the keeper's house and north tower met the same fate. However, two years prior to the 1877 demise of the lights, the optics had been moved to a third pair of lights. The new towers were built of iron plates, lined with brick; the present keeper's house was built at this time.

*(Continued, following pages)*

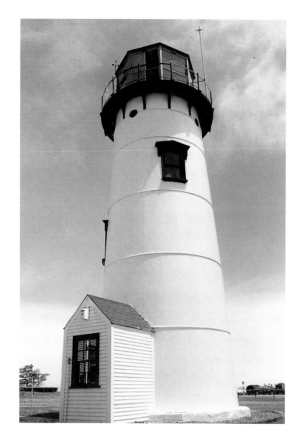

Twin Lights, CHATHAM, Mass.

# Chatham Light

In 1923 the Chatham north light was moved to Eastham's Nauset Beach to replace the Three Sisters Lighthouses, thus ending 115 years of twin lights at Chatham. A new rotating optic was placed in the remaining tower along with an incandescent oil vapor lens. In 1939 the Coast Guard electrified the light, increasing its intensity from 30,000 to 800,000 candlepower. The Fresnel lens and entire lantern room were removed from the Chatham light in 1969 when aero beacons were installed, producing a rotating 2.8 million candlepower light visible for 25 miles. A new, larger lantern room was constructed to accommodate the new optics. The old lantern room and lens are on the grounds of the Chatham Historical Society.

The light was automated in 1982; the keeper's dwelling is used for Coast Guard housing and offices associated with the Coast Guard Station. The monument standing near the foundaton of the old north light was erected in memory of seven members of the Monomoy Life Saving Station who died in a rescue attempt in 1902.

*View from the lantern room*

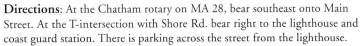

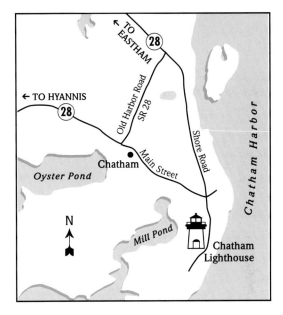

**Directions**: At the Chatham rotary on MA 28, bear southeast onto Main Street. At the T-intersection with Shore Rd. bear right to the lighthouse and coast guard station. There is parking across the street from the lighthouse.

# Nauset Light & The Three Sisters

Following petition by local residents,in 1837 the government decided to establish a lighthouse station at Nauset Beach, on the back shore of Cape Cod halfway between Highland (Cape Cod) Light and the twin lights at Chatham. The decision was not entirely met with enthusiasm as "wrecking" (salvaging materials from wrecked ships) had been a major industry on the Cape for some time. A lighthouse, area residents claimed, would significantly hurt local "business".

To differentiate the new station from its neighbors (Highland and Chatham), a unique plan was devised. Three identical lighthouses were built 150 feet apart, the only "triplet" lighthouses in U.S. history; a one-story keeper's house was also built. The nickname "Three Sisters of Nauset" quickly followed. In 1856 all three were fitted with sixth-order Fresnel lenses and in 1875 a more solid keeper's house added.

By 1890 the Three Sisters stood close to the edge of the bluff and in 1892 three new wooden towers were built further back from the cliff. Fourth-order Fresnel lenses were added, along with a new keeper's house and oil house. In 1911 Nauset was changed to a single light; the center lighthouse was again moved back from the bluff and the two other towers removed and sold.

In 1923 Chatham became a single-light station and the discontinued twin was relocated to Nauset Beach; the keeper's house was moved back next to the new tower. The final Sister was subsequently sold to private owners. The Nauset became a familiar Cape Cod icon and trade-mark logo when the top half of the white cast-iron tower was painted red in 1941.

*Original lens, now at the Eastham Visitors Center*

Nauset light was automated in 1955, the Fresnel lens replaced by aerobeacons; the characteristic changed to alternating red and white flashes in 1981. The Coast Guard proposed the decommissioning of the lighthouse in 1993 as erosion had almost completely destroyed the cliff just east of the tower. The Nauset Light Preservation Society was formed, spearheaded by local residents, and in 1995 a long-term lease was granted for the lighthouse. Federal grant money and individual contributions funded the move to the present site in the fall of 1996. In the fall of 1998 the house was relocated next to the lighthouse.

The old Fresnel lens is on display at the Cape Cod National Seashore Visitors Center in Eastham. The keeper's house is now owned by the National Park Service and leased to private owner. The light is now a private aid to navigation.

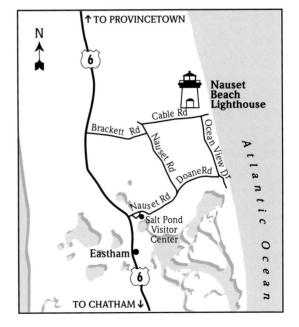

**Directions:** See directions for the Three Sisters, following page.

*First Sister*

*Second Sister*

*Third Sister*

The National Park Service has purchased and restored the Three Sisters to their original configuration at a site about one-third mile from the Nauset light. A well-marked path leads from the beach parking area to the small park.

# The Three Sisters

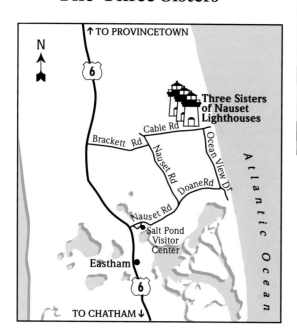

C. 1906

**Directions: (For Nauset Light & Three Sisters)**

Follow RT 6 into Eastham and turn east on Brackett Rd. (marked with "Nauset Beach Light" sign). Continue to Nauset Rd. and turn left, then bear right onto Cable Rd. Continue to the road's end at the intersection with Ocean View Drive and beach parking area. Across Ocean View Dr. there is a marked path leading to the restored lighthouses.

Or.. From RT 6 turn right at a "Cape Cod National Seashore" sign onto Nauset/Salt Pond Rd. Pass the Salt Pond Visitor Center and continue on to Ocean View Dr. Turn left at that intersection and continue to the Nauset Beach parking area.

# Highland (Cape Cod) Light

A preponderance of shipwrecks at the "High Land" prompted the Boston Marine Society recommendation in the late 1700s that a lighthouse be built at this location in North Truro. In 1791 a 30-foot brick lighthouse was built 500 feet from the edge of the bluff. To avoid confusion with Boston Light, Highland Light became the first lighthouse in the nation with a flashing light.

One of the worst wrecks near the light was that of the British bark *Josephus* in 1852. Keeper Enoch Hamilton returned hours after the wreck to find that two of the 16 crew members had washed ashore and survived. One of the survivors, John Jasper, later became the captain of an ocean liner; when his vessel passed Highland light he would dip the flag as a signal of respect to the keeper. (*Continued on following page*)

C. 1917

# Highland Light

A new Highland Light was built in 1857 and equipped with a first-order Fresnel lens. This powerful light made Highland one of the coast's most powerful; it was also the highest on the New England mainland. In 1901 an even larger Fresnel lens, floating on a bed of mercury, was installed. When an electric light was put inside this lens in 1932, Highland then became the coast's most powerful beacon. The four million candlepower light was visible for 45 miles (reportedly for 75 miles in clear weather).

In the early 1950s the giant lens was removed and replaced by aerobeacons; the light was automated in 1986 and the keeper's house used for Coast Guard housing. The lighthouse now belongs to the National Park Service and is considered a private aid to navigation. Signs on Cape Cod Route 6 direct you to the lighthouse, now located at the Highland Golf Links.

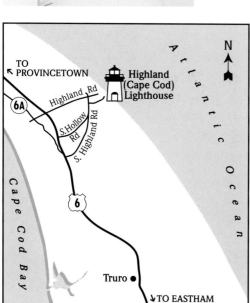

**Directions:** Take US Rt 6 to North Truro; turn east at the "Highland (Cape Cod) Light" sign and follow Highland Road to a T-intersection with South Highland Rd. Turn right and follow South Highland to Lighthouse Rd., turn left at the entrance to the Cape Cod lighthouse (marked) and Highland Golf Links. There is a parking area at the light. It is now possible to walk all around the lighthouse since its relocation in the fall of 1996. Because the lighthouse is located on the golf course, following signs to "Highland Golf Links" also bring you to the lighthouse.

# Relocating a Lighthouse

The first Highland lighthouse was built 500 feet from the edge of a 125-foot cliff. Erosion claimed at least three feet of the cliff per year until, by the early 1990s, the lighthouse stood barely 100 feet from the edge. In 1990 alone, 40 feet were lost just north of the lighthouse. A group within the Truro Historical Society began fund raising for relocation of the light.

Donations from local residents and tourists, coupled with sales of Highland Light memorabilia, raised $150,000. In 1996, this money combined with National Park Service, state and Coast Guard funds totalled $1.5 million, the amount needed for relocation of the 404-ton lighthouse to a site 450 feet back from its original location.

The operation got underway in June 1996 and took 18 days to complete. The relocated lighthouse now stands close to the seventh fairway of the Highland Golf Links. On Sunday, November 7, 1996 Highland Light was relighted amid pomp and ceremony.

*Plans for the relocation--International Chimney, contractors*

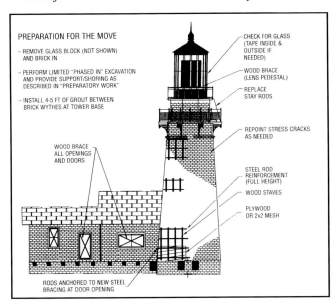

# Wood End Light

The 39-foot square brick tower that still stands at Wood End was built in 1872, making it the youngest lighthouse in the Provincetown area. The lighthouse originally was painted brown and exhibited a red flashing light. In 1896 a second wooden keeper's house was added, along with an oil house. A fog bell in a tower was added near the light in 1902.

Duty at this station had its unique drawbacks as the keeper in 1880 complained of the "stench and flies coming from the fish-oil works" between Wood End and Long Point, a mile away. Also notable was the 1927 collision of a Navy submarine and Coast Guard cutter eight days before Christmas one-half mile south of Wood End light; 42 men perished in the disaster.

The lighthouse was automated in 1961 with all outbuildings except the oil house destroyed. The fifth-order Fresnel lens was removed and replaced by an aerobeacon; the light was converted to solar power in 1981. It is possible to walk across the breakwater, then over sand to the lighthouse, although at high tide several low points are covered with water, making the route tricky. Excursion boats and whale watches also pass by this light.

Wood End Light, Provincetown, Mass.

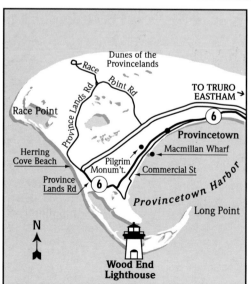

**Directions:** The light can be seen in the distance from the Pilgrim's Landing Plaque area at the end of Commercial Street (one way), opposite the breakwater that extends to the lighthouse. Whale watching cruises from Provincetown pass close to this light and offer good views. To walk to the lighthouse, park at the breakwater at the end of Commercial St. The breakwater is about 1/2 mile long; the lighthouse is another 1/2 mile to your right over sand. Be prepared for a strenuous walk; you will be crossing through water at several points unless the tide is dead low.

# Long Point Light

At the fingertip of the curling arm of Cape Cod, Long Point was a settlement of about 200 people in the 1800s, boasting a school and sea salt industry. Provincetown had become a major fishing port and it was decided a lighthouse at Long Point would aid mariners entering the harbor. In 1827 the first lighthouse was completed and consisted of a lantern room atop the keeper's house; a sixth-order Fresnel lens was installed in 1856.

During the Civil War a Confederate warship was seen near Provincetown, prompting the construction of two forts at Long Point, close to the lighthouse. Local residents called the batteries "Fort Useless" and "Fort Harmless"; no shots were ever fired.

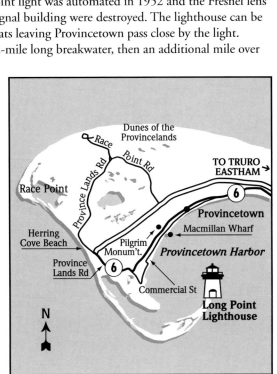

A new 38-foot brick lighthouse and keeper's house were built in 1875 with a fog bell and fifth-order Fresnel lens installed at that time. Long Point light was automated in 1952 and the Fresnel lens replaced; solar panels were added in 1982. The keeper's house and fog signal building were destroyed. The lighthouse can be seen in the distance from MacMillan Wharf in Provincetown; various boats leaving Provincetown pass close by the light. Walking to the lighthouse is possible but involves crossing an uneven 1/2-mile long breakwater, then an additional mile over sand to the point, crossing through water unless at dead low tide.

**Directions:** From US Route 6, take either of the exits west into Provincetown and head to MacMillan Wharf. Provincetown is a congested area with narrow streets; parking is available at the wharf and all whale watching cruises depart from that area. Long Point light can be seen from the wharf; the whale watching excursions all pass close to this light. To walk to the lighthouse, park at the breakwater at the end of Commercial St. The breakwater is about 1/2 mile long; the lighthouse is another mile to your left over sand to Long Point. Be prepared for a strenuous walk; you will be crossing through water at several points unless the tide is dead low.

91

# Race Point Light

Countless shipwrecks occured in the area of Race Point at the northern tip of Cape Cod throughout the 18th century, as all vessels travelling between Boston and points south had to negotiate the treacherous bars off the point. As early as 1808 the people of Provincetown asked for a lighthouse at Race Point; the first was built in 1816. The rubblestone tower's revolving light was an attempt to differentiate it from the other lighthouses on the Cape, and one of the earliest of this design.

In 1852 a fog bell was installed and three years later a fourth-order Frensel lens added. The fog bell was replaced in 1873 with a steam-driven fog signal housed in a new building. The old stone tower was replaced in 1875 with a 45-foot cast iron structure, lined with brick; the Fresnel lens was moved and changed from flashing white to fixed. Three keepers and their families lived in two separate keeper's houses; the children's walk to school was 2.5 miles over sand each day, each way.

Despite the help afforded by the lighthouse, lives continued to be lost in the Race Point vicinity. During the period 1890 to 1903 there were 28 major shipping disasters in the area. The infamous Portland Gale of 1898 claimed more than 500 lives, 200 on the steamer *Portland*. Pieces of some wrecks continue to appear occasionally in the area as the sands shift.

92

During the early 1800s a sizeable fishing community and saltworks flourished at Race Point. The small community, known as "Helltown" even declared a separate school district in the 1830s. However, the latter part of the 19th century saw the fishing settlement dwindle.

Race Point light was electrified in 1957 and three years later the larger keeper's house razed. The light was automated in 1978, a new optic replaced the Fresnel lens and solar power subsequently installed. Now on the grounds of the Cape Cod National Seashore, the surrounding property, keeper's house and oil house were leased to the New England Lighthouse Foundation. Repairs and restoration to the interior and exterior were completed in 1997. Overnight stays in the keeper's house are now possible during summer months.

Parking is available at Race Point Beach. The walk to the light is strenuous, two miles over sand. A four-wheel drive vehicle and permit are required for access to the restricted area. Dune tours are possible in the summer months.

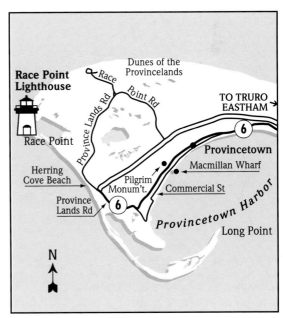

**Directions:** Take the Race Point exit from Route 6 and follow the road through the Provincelands park area. Bear right at the Provincetown Airport and pass the visitors center. The road ends in a parking area at Race Point Beach. The lighthouse is a two-mile walk over sand from the parking area. Access is possible with four-wheel drive vehicle but an over-sand permit and check in is required. Alternatively, the light can be seen at a distance from the parking area at Herring Cove Beach. Whale watching cruises from Provincetown pass close to this light and offer good views.

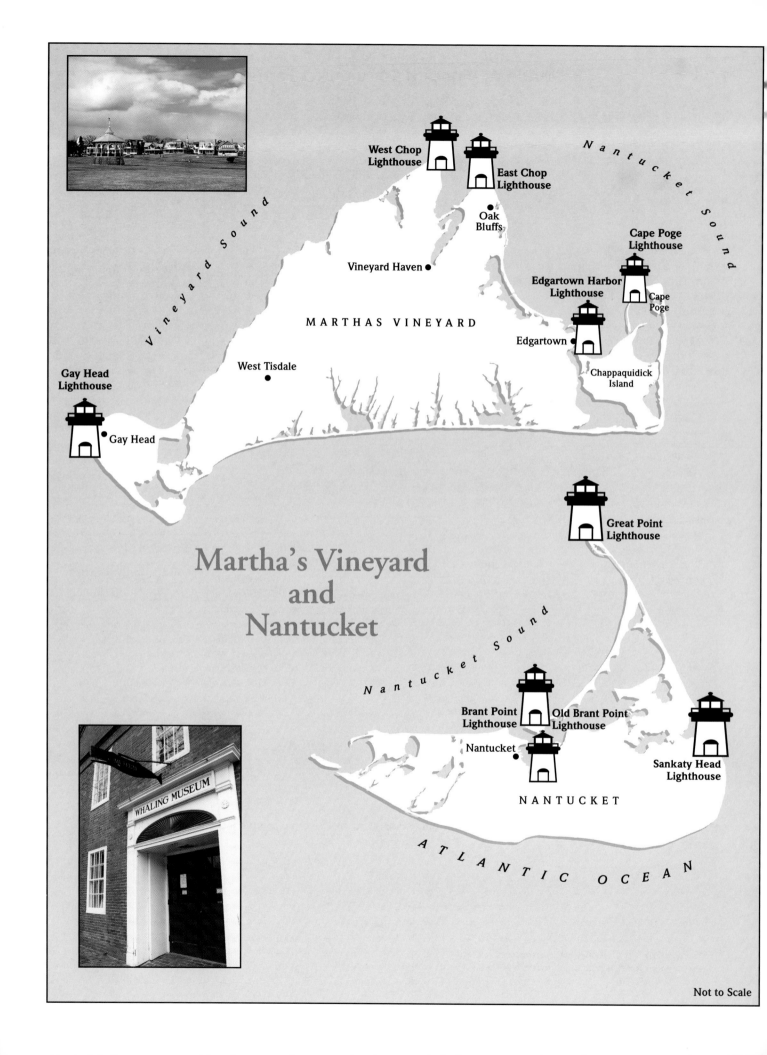

West Chop
Lighthouse

East Chop
Lighthouse

Oak
Bluffs

Nantucket Sound

Cape Poge
Lighthouse

Vineyard Sound

Vineyard Haven

Edgartown Harbor
Lighthouse

Cape
Poge

MARTHAS VINEYARD

Edgartown

Gay Head
Lighthouse

West Tisdale

Chappaquidick
Island

Gay Head

Great Point
Lighthouse

Martha's Vineyard
and
Nantucket

Nantucket Sound

Brant Point
Lighthouse

Old Brant Point
Lighthouse

Nantucket

Sankaty Head
Lighthouse

NANTUCKET

WHALING MUSEUM

ATLANTIC OCEAN

Not to Scale

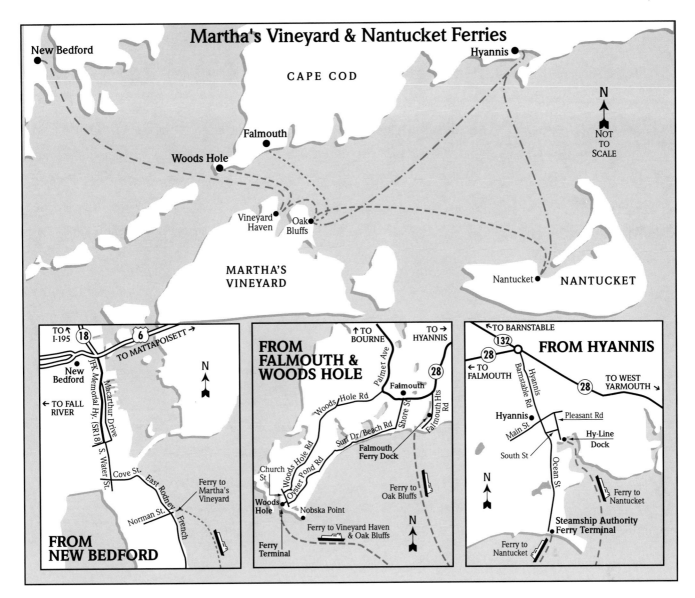

## MARTHA'S VINEYARD FERRIES

**From Woods Hole:** From MA 28 (Palmer Ave.) in Falmouth, turn onto Woods Hole Rd., following the signs to "Vineyard Ferry". Turn left, crossing the bridge to the Woods Hole parking lot and ferry terminal. There is a parking area on Palmer Street if the Woods Hole lot is full (a sign will so indicate); there is shuttle bus service to the ferry. Reservations are required for an automobile. The Woods Hole ferry operates year 'round to Vineyard Haven and Oak Bluffs; crossing time is 45 minutes. **Martha's Vineyard & Nantucket Steamship Authority, P.O. Box 284, Woods Hole, MA 02543 (508) 693- 9130** For automobile reservations: **(508) 477-8600**

**From Falmouth:** Follow MA 28 into Falmouth (MA 28 is Main St.). Turn south onto Falmouth Heights Road; the ferry dock is about 0.25 mile, just south of Robbins Rd. The Falmouth Ferry operates to Oak Bluffs from late May to mid-October; crossing time is 45 minutes. **Island Commuter Corp. 75 Falmouth Heights Rd., Falmouth, MA 02540 (508) 548-4800.** **Ferry service to Martha's Vineyard is also available from Hyannis and New Bedford. Both operate only seasonally mid May to late October.

## NANTUCKET FERRIES

Ferry transportation to Nantucket is available from Hyannis and Woods Hole. In Hyannis the Hy-Line Cruise dock is on Ocean Street; the Steamship Authority ferry terminal is off South St. just past Pleasant St. Both companies offer parking and private lots also are available nearby. Departure times for both ferries allow sufficient time on the island to visit the lighthouses, but taking a car to the island is not advised. **Hy-Line Cruises, Ocean St. Dock, Hyannis, MA. 02601 (508) 778-2600 (information) (508) 778-2602 (reservations). Steamship Authority: P.O. Box 284 Woods Hole, MA 02543 Reservations: (508)- 477-8600 Information: (508) 228-0262**

# West Chop Light

The harbor at Vineyard Haven on Martha's Vineyard is protected by two areas of land known as East Chop and West Chop. The first 25-foot stone tower at West Chop was built in 1817; the town was then called Holmes Hole and the light often referred to as Holmes Hole Light. In 1843 inspection found the house in poor condition and the decision was made to build a new house and rubblestone tower in 1846, almost 1000 feet southeast of the original location.

Three range lights were added in 1854, replaced in 1856 by a range light on the keeper's house which was then discontinued in 1859. A steam-driven fog signal was added in 1882; an assistant keeper's house also was built during that year.

By 1891 the proliferation of large homes in the area began to obscure the light and a 17-foot mast with the light on top was added. Soon after, the tower was replaced by a new 45-foot brick tower, painted red. The new West Chop light was painted white in 1896. The light was automated in 1976 but the original fourth-order Fresnel lens remains in place. The Vineyard Environmental Research Institute uses the buildings at the station. The lighthouse can be seen from West Chop Road and on entering Vineyard Haven harbor on the ferries.

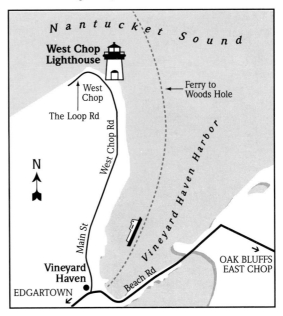

**Directions: From the Vineyard Haven ferry landing,** turn right onto Main St. and continue to West Chop Rd. Follow West Chop Rd. (becomes one way) to the lighthouse. Parking is possible on the street, NOT in the drive. Continuing past the lighthouse the road becomes Loop Rd. which eventually winds around back into Vineyard Haven.

**From Oak Bluffs,** follow Beach Rd. into Vineyard Haven, then take Main St./West Chop Rd. to the lighthouse. Bus tours of the island also are available from the Vineyard Haven ferry landing but these are not primarily lighthouse tours.

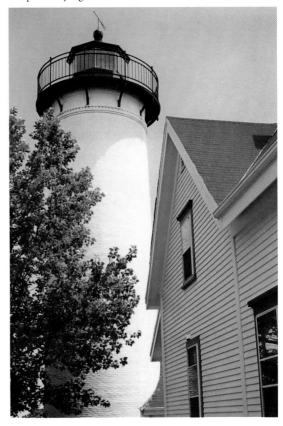

# East Chop Light

In 1869 Captain Silas Daggett erected a lighthouse at East Chop, the eastern point of Vineyard Haven Harbor, and operated it privately for seven years. Donations from local merchants paid for upkeep of the light. This structure burnedin 1871 but Daggett rebuilt it as a light atop a house. The government purchased the land and lighthouse in 1878 and built a new keeper's house and present cast-iron structure.

The keeper's house and oil house were removed in 1934 when the station was automated. The original Fresnel lens was replaced by a plastic lens in 1984. From 1962 to 1984 the lighthouse was painted a reddish-brown, earning it the nickname "Chocolate Lighthouse". Today only the tower remains, painted a more traditional white and exhibiting a three-second green flash, visible for 15 miles.

*Oak Bluffs*

EAST CHOP LIGHT, OAK BLUFFS, MASS.

In 1986 the Vineyard Environmental Research Institute became responsible for the maintenance of East Chop light. The license was transferred to the Dukes County Historical Society in 1993, along with licenses for Gay Head and Edgartown Harbor lights. The Society periodically opens the lights to the public in summer months.

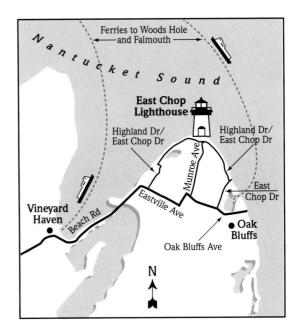

**Directions:** From Vineyard Haven ferry landing, bear left onto Beach Rd. ; follow the "East Chop Light" signs, bearing left onto Eastville Ave. then right onto East Chop Dr./Highland Dr. Continue along the shore to the light. From Oak Bluffs, follow Oak Bluffs Drive to East Chop Drive. Turn right and follow East Chop Dr./Highland Dr. to the light. The lighthouse is at a park area with limited street parking.

## Gay Head Light

Built in 1798 to aid mariners entering Vineyard Sound from Buzzard's Bay, Gay Head lighthouse stands in one of the most picturesque locations in New England, atop the 130-foot multicolored clay cliffs at the western shore of Martha's Vineyard. The original octagonal lighthouse was first lighted in November 1799.

In 1838 the lantern and deck were rebuilt; subsequently conflicting reports and recommendations were submitted regarding the visibility of the light. Finally, in 1854, a new, 51-foot brick lighthouse was built to house a first-order Fresnel lens which contained 1008 prisms. However, despite the new, powerful light, shipwrecks continued to happen regularly in the vicinity. The worst of these disasters occurred in the early morning of January 19, 1884 when the passenger steamer

*City of Columbus* ran aground on Devil's Bridge, a treacherous ledge near the Gay Head Cliffs. Twenty minutes later 100 people on board had drowned. Fortunately some managed to hold onto the rigging long enough for the lighthouse keeper to arrive in a lifeboat with a crew of Gay Head Indians. The wreck of the *City of Columbus* remains among New England's worst marine disasters.

*The original Fresnel lens, now displayed in Edgartown*

The brick keeper's house was torn down in 1856 as it was thought to be the extreme dampness of the house which was causing an often fatal mysterious illness. In 1902 a new wooden structure was built on a much higher foundation so it would remain dry. In 1952 the old Fresnel lens was replaced by a modern automatic light.

The lens can be seen today on the grounds of the Dukes County Historical Society in Edgartown. Today only the lighthouse tower remains at Gay Head; it is easily accessible by car with parking available at a scenic lookout area. The Historical Society periodically opens the lighthouse.

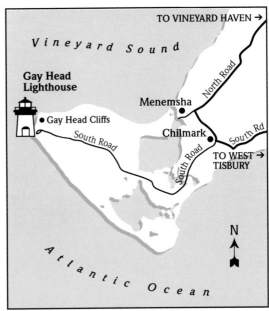

**Directions:** Follow appropriate signs to West Tisbury and Chilmark--you will be following North Rd. (from Vineyard Haven) or South Road (from West Tisbury). At Chilmark continue on South Rd. to Gay Head; signs clearly indicate the route to Gay Head. The lighthouse is at the road's end. A parking and refreshment area is available.

101

# Edgartown Harbor Light

Martha's Vineyard had a prosperous whaling industry in the early 19th century and the harbor at Edgartown was one of the island's most protected. In 1828 the government purchased land and a two-story house with lantern on the roof was built for about $4000. The fixed white light was visible for 14 miles. This type of lighthouse structure was commonly known as "Cape Cod style"; today no such structures survive on Cape Cod save the much-changed Bass River lighthouse.

Edgartown Harbor light was located offshore on a stone pier; in 1830 a causeway was built to the lighthouse. The walkway became known locally as the "Bridge of Sighs" because men about to leave on whaling voyages often strolled there with girlfriends or wives.

The lighthouse and walkway were damaged and repaired many times but the Hurricane of '38 was the final blow and in 1939 the Coast Guard demolished Edgartown Light. Plans were to erect a beacon on a skeleton tower but objections from residents prompted an alternate plan: relocation of an 1873 cast iron tower from Crane's Beach in Ipswich. The 45-foot tower received an automatic light flashing red every six seconds.

A new plastic lens was installed in 1990 when the light was converted to solar power. The Dukes County Historical Society did major work to refurbish the light in 1995. Over time sand gradually filled in the area between the lighthouse and the mainland so that today Edgartown Harbor light is on a beach.

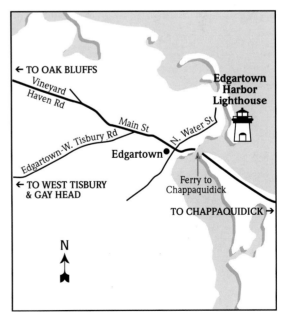

## Directions:

Follow signs to Edgartown (via Vineyard Haven Rd. or West Tisbury-Edgartown Rd.) From Main Street in Edgartown turn left (north) onto North Water Street and continue to past the Chappaquiddick Ferry landing. The lighthouse is at the tip of a sandy beach area and marina. Edgartown is a congested area and street parking is often difficult; the lighthouse is a short walk from most anywhere in town.

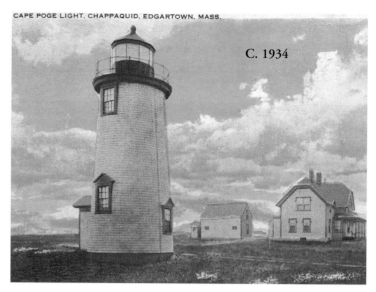

C. 1934

# Cape Poge Light

Cape Poge is an exposed, windswept point at the northeast tip of Chappaquiddick, an island immediately east of Martha's Vineyard. This lighthouse runs a close second to Nantucket's Brant Point as the New England lighthouse rebuilt and relocated the most times. At least five towers have been built at this location and there have been several moves.

The first 35-foot wooden Cape Poge Lighthouse was built in 1801; the tower exhibited a fixed white light 55 feet above sea level. Although records indicate some sort of previous beacon at the site, little is known of it. President Thomas Jefferson appointed Thomas Mayhew the first keeper at Cape Poge, where he and nine other family members lived for 34 years. After Mayhew's death in 1834 his successor couldn't reach the station for two weeks due to ice. During that time a schooner was wrecked on Cape Poge, claiming several lives.

In 1838 a new tower was built further back from the edge of the eroding bluff but by 1844 its poor condition required that a new tower be constructed. A fourth-order Fresnel lens was added in 1857. By 1878 the keeper's house was threatened by the sea; a new, larger house was built and a new lighthouse constructed in 1880. A new wooden tower, 40 feet inland from the old one, was built in 1893. Although intended as a temporary structure, that tower is still standing.

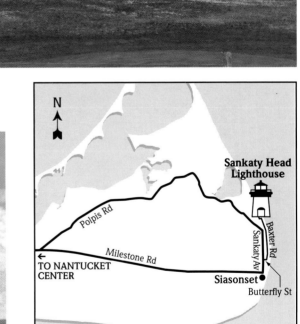

An estimate by the Army Corps of Engineers in 1990 predicted Sankaty Head Light would be in danger of falling over the eroding bluff within 10 years. In 1991, concerned islanders formed a nonprofit group to raise funds for the relocation of the tower. However, during recent years erosion control measures have been successful, delaying the inevitable move or extinction of the lighthouse. Renovations to the tower were done in 1994 but the house and other outbuildings have been removed.

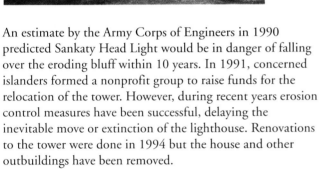

**Directions**: From Nantucket Center, follow the signs "To Airport, Siasconset". At the rotary, continue onto Milestone St (follow "To Siasconset" directionals). Follow this road about 8 miles to the village and a small rotary. Continue around the rotary, bearing left into Main St. At the street's end, turn left onto what becomes Sankaty Ave. Turn right onto Butterfly Lane, then left at the T-intersection with Baxter St; the lighthouse is at the end of Baxter St. There is limited parking and the area is thickly settled.

# Great Point Light

Before the completion of the Cape Cod Canal in 1914, the stretch between Great Point and Monomoy was one of the busiest sections of the Atlantic coast. The residents of Nantucket first petitioned for a lighthouse in 1770, but not until 1784 did the General Court of Massachusetts agree to the request. The first wooden tower was completed in that same year. For almost 30 years there was no keeper's house at Great Point, so the keepers had to reach the station on foot or horseback, a distance of seven miles. In 1812 a dwelling was constructed but in 1816 the original lighthouse was destroyed by fire. A new stone tower was completed in 1818.

In 1857 Great Point light was fitted with a Fresnel lens, the tower lined with brick and an assistant keeper's house built. Despite the improved light, between 1863 and 1890 there were 43 shipwrecks near the lighthouse; confusion of Great Point light with the Cross Rip lightship was cited.

The son of the last keeper at Great Point remembered seeing packages dropped from a plane one Christmas. Having no idea what they were, the boy hesitated in opening the packages but found they were filled with presents and books. The man who dropped the bundles was Edward Rowe Snow, popular historian and "Flying Santa" to lighthouse keepers.

*"The lighthouse was not sold,*
*It was very, very old.*
*This is the new one,*
*It shines like the sun.*
*It is located near a bush,*
*The old one got smushed."*

Ten-year old student,
Nantucket Elementary School

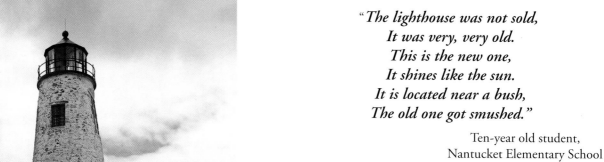

Great Point light was automated in the 1950s, and in 1968 the keeper's house razed by a suspicious fire, leaving the old stone tower alone at the site. Erosion brought the sea perilously close to the lighthouse and in 1984 a severe storm destroyed the structure, leaving pile of rubble.

Federal money was allocated for building of a new Great Point light; in 1986 a replica, 300 yards west of the old tower, was completed at a cost of more than one million dollars (more than 200 times the cost of the original 1818 tower). The new solar-powered light is visible for 12 miles. Great Point is now part of Coatue Wildlife Refuge and much of the area is off limits. There is an access fee and four-wheel drive vehicle required for the seven-mile over sand route.

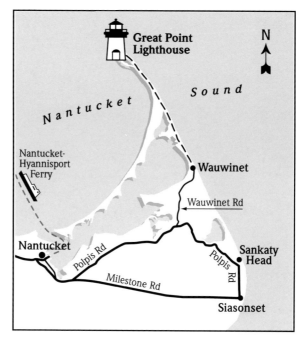

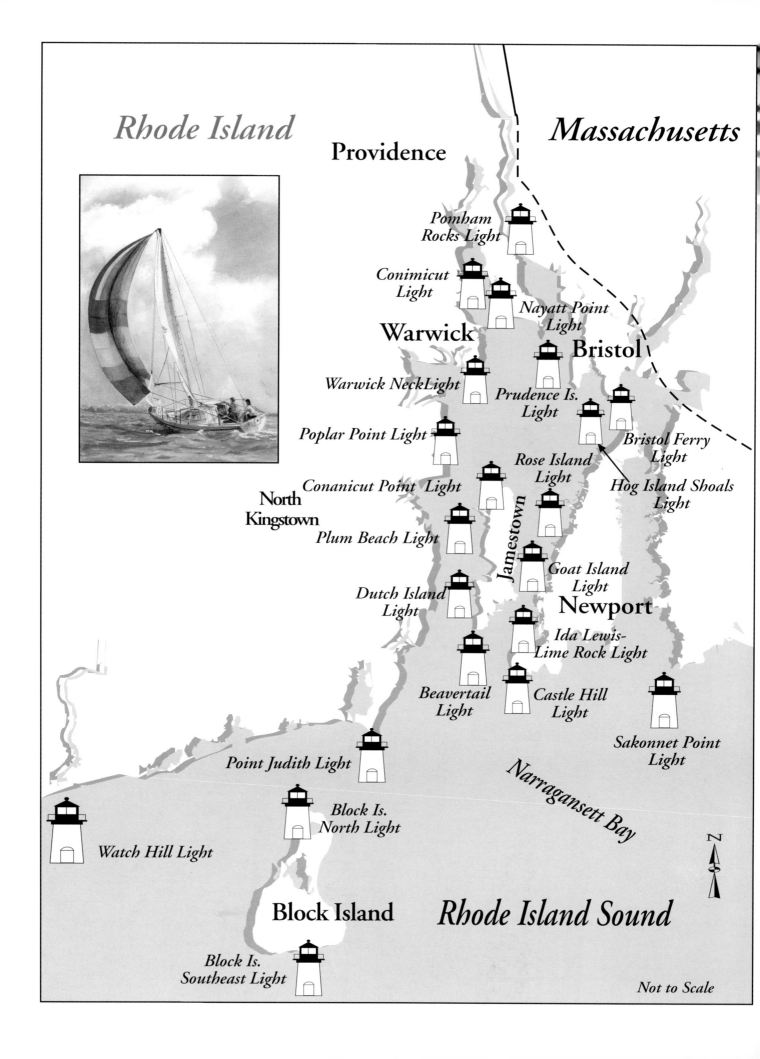

Rhode Island

Providence

*Massachusetts*

Pomham
Rocks Light

Conimicut
Light

Nayatt Point
Light

Warwick

Bristol

Warwick Neck Light

Prudence Is.
Light

Poplar Point Light

Bristol Ferry
Light

Rose Island
Light

Hog Island Shoals
Light

Conanicut Point Light

North
Kingstown

Jamestown

Plum Beach Light

Goat Island
Light

Dutch Island
Light

Newport

Ida Lewis-
Lime Rock Light

Beavertail
Light

Castle Hill
Light

Sakonnet Point
Light

Point Judith Light

*Narragansett Bay*

Block Is.
North Light

N

Watch Hill Light

Block Island

*Rhode Island Sound*

Block Is.
Southeast Light

*Not to Scale*

# The Rhode Island Lighthouse Tradition

*Compiled by Ted Panayotoff*

The State of Rhode Island, also originally known as the Providence Plantations, is a small state, only 37 miles wide by 48 miles long, but with approximately 400 miles of ocean shoreline. Narragansett Bay, with four major rivers flowing into it, is the state's major coastal feature. The numerous islands, coves and small harbors provide many locations where lighthouses and beacons were built during the state's long maritime history. Early on, Rhode Island, often called the "Gateway to Southern New England", developed maritime trade, shipbuilding and fishing industries. Lighthouses played a significant role in the development of those industries by guiding vessels safely in and out of ports.

As early as 1738 the Providence Plantation (Rhode Island) authorized construction of a lighthouse at Beavertail on the southern point of Conanicut Island which divides southern Narragansett Bay. Although not conclusive, there is some evidence that a beacon may have been established at that location as early as 1712 which would make it the oldest lighted aid to navigation in the United States, older than Boston Light established in 1716. In spite of being authorized in 1738, the Beavertail lighthouse wasn't completed until 1749, thus becoming the third oldest colonial lighthouse in the American Colonies.

A little less than 100 years later, in 1843, Rhode Island had nine lighthouses. These early Rhode Island beacons included the seacoast lights at Watch Hill (1808) and Point Judith (1810) which reflected the early emphasis by the Lighthouse Service on construction of coastal and landfall lights. Harbor lights followed, with Newport Harbor (Goat Island) lighted in 1824 and Wickford Harbor (Poplar Point) in 1831. Of the remaining four early Rhode Island lighthouses, one marked the north end of Block Island (1829) and three served to aid navigation up Narragansett Bay: Dutch Island (1826), Warwick Neck (1827) and Nayatt Point(1828).

When the U.S. Lighthouse Service was reorganized under the Lighthouse Board in 1852, additional Rhode Island light stations quickly followed to mark harbors and aid navigation in Narragansett Bay: Prudence Island (1852), Brenton Reef Lighthship station (1853), Lime Rock (1854) and Bristol Ferry (1855). In the early 1870s navigation in the Upper Bay and Providence River was addressed with five lights. Three of these were light-houses with resident keepers at the station (Bullock's Point, 1872, Sabine Point, 1871, and Pomham Rocks, 1871) and two were beacons tended by a nonresident keeper (Sassafras Point, 1872 and Fuller's Ledge, 1872). Pomham Rocks is the only of these lights still standing. During this period Rose Island Light, off Newport, also was added in 1870.

In the next 20 years (1881 to 1901), ten more lighthouses were built in Rhode Island, all but one in Narragansett Bay. Five were cast iron caisson-style structures typical of the period. Bristol Ferry, Hog Island Shoal and Brenton Reef lighthouses all were initially lightship stations, with the Texas-tower-style Brenton Reef light the last constructed in the state (1962). A number of experiments with fog signal equipment were tested at the Beavertail location as was the use of coal gas as an illuminate. Although reported to have been technically successful, the local inventor's work ran afoul of strong whale oil interests and was not pursued.

Time and nature have not been kind to Rhode Island's lighthouses. Of the 31built only 21 still remain; the infamous New England Hurricane of 1938 was especially destructive . Whale Rock light was completely destroyed and the keeper killed, all station structures at Prudence Island were lost save the lighthouse tower, the Warwick Neck tower had to be moved after severe erosion . Two other locations were discontinued following severe damage. Members of the keeper's family were killed at Prudence Island and Beavertail Lights.

Today many of Rhode Island's remaining lighthouses are listed on the National Register and are cared for by various non-profit organization or private owners.  Efforts are underway to save  those structures which are endangered in order to preserve the state's maritime tradition.

# Pomham Rocks Light

Perched on a small island located on the east side of the Providence River, 800 feet from shore, Pomham Rocks light was named for a Narragansett Indian Chief. The lighthouse was put into operation on December 1, 1871 with a sixth-order Fresnel lens. The style of the structure is similar to that of Rose Island light, a square wood-framed two-story building with the second level supporting the tower and lantern room.

A continuous fog siren was installed at the station in 1900, but complaints from nearby residents prompted the change to a three-second blast at 12-second intervals. In 1903 a fog bell replaced the siren. The original sixth-order Fresnel lens was replaced by a fourth order lens in 1939. That lens was later removed in 1974 and donated to the Custom House Maritime Museum in Newburyport, MA; it is on display there now.

Pomham Rocks light was discontinued in 1974 and replaced by a light on a skeleton tower. Abandoned by the Coast Guard, the government sold the property in 1980 to the Mobil Oil Company. For a time there were resident caretakers on the island, but there are none at present. Mobil Oil still cares for the property. Good views are possible from the East Bay Bicycle Path that follows the Providence River, but best views are from the water.

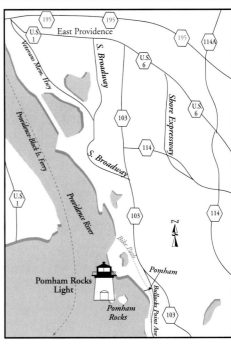

**Directions:** Take Exit 4 (Route 103, Veteran's Mem. Pkwy) off I-95. Follow the Parkway about 5 miles to the Bullocks Point Rd. parking area for the East Bay Bike Path. The lighthouse is offshore and can be seen from the path.

# Nayatt Point Light

A dangerous shoal off Conimicut Point, near the mouth of the Providence River, was a danger to mariners. The first lighthouse at Nayatt Point, built in 1828, was intended to guide vessels past this danger. Attached to the present brick dwelling, the 23-foot brick tower wasn't well built and was severely damaged by a storm in 1855. A new 25-foot tower was completed in 1856 and attached to the original keeper's house. Rhode Island's oldest standing keeper's dwelling, the 1828 structure has never been altered or rebuilt, although there have been additions to the structure.

The 1863 fourth-order Fresnel lens had a focal plane only 31 feet above the river, prompting the decision to build a new lighthouse on the shoal off Conimicut Point to better warn mariners away from the dangerous point and to guide them into the Providence River. The dwelling at Nayatt Point was used by the keepers at Conimicut Point; the "commute" was a one-mile row to and from the light for duty. In 1890 a new, sparkplug-style light was built at Conimicut Point and the Nayatt Point property sold to private ownership. The property has recently again been sold in 2001.

A Fresnel lens from a lightship is now in the lantern room but the light is not an aid to navigation. Best views are by boat although this light and the Conimicut Point light can be seen from the nearby beach.

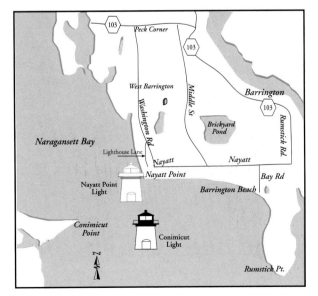

**Directions:** Take RI 103 or 103/114 (From Warren) into Barrington. At the intersection with Rumstick Rd., turn south and continue to Nayatt Rd. Turn onto Nayatt Rd, continue to Bay Rd. and turn left. Nayatt Point is approxmiately 2 miles west on the beach; the lighthouse can be seen at a distance. Best views are from the water via excursion boats from Warren, RI.

# Conimicut Light

In 1868 a granite tower on this ledge was built to replace Nayatt Point light by better marking the dangerous Conimicut Point Shoal. A fourth-order Fresnel lens showed a fixed white light. Until a keeper's house was built on the pier at the light, keepers made the one-mile row to and from quarters at Nayatt Point. Unfortunately, large chunks of rapidly moving ice on the Providence River struck the pier in March, 1875 destroying the keeper's dwelling. Thereafter, the house at Nayatt Point was permanently used by the Conimicut keepers.

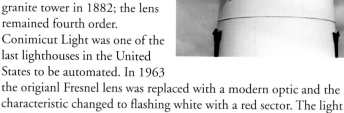

A new cast-iron sparkplug style caisson structure replaced the granite tower in 1882; the lens remained fourth order.

Conimicut Light was one of the last lighthouses in the United States to be automated. In 1963 the origianl Fresnel lens was replaced with a modern optic and the characteristic changed to flashing white with a red sector. The light can be viewed distantly from Conimicut Point Park in Warwick and from the area near Nayatt Point. Best views are from the water.

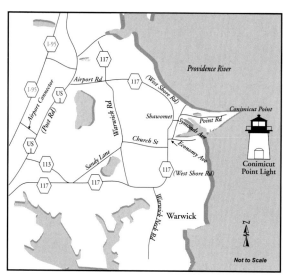

**Directions:** If coming **from Warwick**, follow Rt. 117(west Shore Rd) north/ northeast to the intersection with Economy Ave. Turn right (east) onto Economy Ave, then left into Symonds Ave. Continue to Point Ave, turn right and continue to the park entrance. **From I-95 or US RT. 1:** Take Exit 13 off I-95 to Airport Access Rd and continue to the intersection with US 1 (Post Rd.). Turn north (left)onto Post Rd.; at the intersection with Airport Rd., turn right (east). Follow the road past the intersection with Rt. 117a (Warwick Ave) and into Rt 117 (West Shore Rd). Turn left (east) onto Economy Ave, then left onto Symonds Ave. Continue to Point Ave., turn right and follow the road to the park entrance. The lighthouse is offshore.

The light can also be seen offshore from the Barrington Town Beach (see previous page). Excursion cruises from Warren, RI. offer closer views.

# Prudence Island (Sandy Point) Light

Built in 1823, this structure is Rhode Island's oldest lighthouse. The octagonal, granite lighthouse at Prudence Island initially stood on the southern tip of Goat Island in Newport Harbor. In 1851 the 25-foot tower and lantern room were dismantled and relocated to Sandy Point on Prudence Island. The island, about six miles long and three miles wide, is located in Narragansett Bay; dangerous hidden ledges known as Halfway Rocks are located in the waters between Prudence Island and the mainland.

The keeper's house was located 190 feet west of the lighthouse with an elevated walkway connecting the tower and dwelling. In 1857, the original Winslow Lewis lighting apparatus was replaced by a fifth-order Fresnel lens. Aa fog bell was added in 1885 and a boathouse in 1895. A testament to sound construction, the lighthouse tower

withstood the hurricane of 1938 which reduced the keeper's house to rubble. A fourth-order lens was installed in 1939 and the light electrified; it was automated in 1961 and a 250mm modern lens is now in the lantern room.

An old deed to the lightstation stipulated that the property was to be given to President Millard Fillmore, and thenceforth handed down to each succeeding president of the United States. Although other lighthouses have been associated with specific presidents--Kennedy, Bush(both), Roosevelt-- this structure apparently has an official claim to be the "President's Lighthouse". The island is reached by ferry from Bristol; the lighthouse is about a mile walk from the landing.

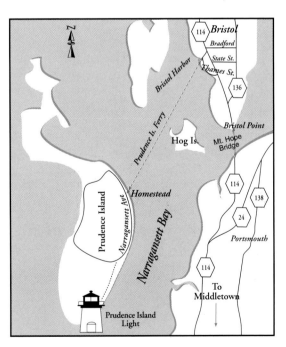

**Directions:** A ferry to the island departs from Bristol. In Bristol, take any cross street (State, Bradford) to Thames St. The ferry is at the Church St. wharf. From the ferry landing at Homestead on Prudence Is., follow Narragansett Ave. south for about 1 mile; take the first left to Sandy Point and the lighthouse.

# Bristol Ferry Light

Marking the narrow passage between Mount Hope Bay and Narragansett Bay, this light was first established in 1855, partially in response to a petition to the Lighthouse Board by captain of the steamer *Bay State*. Vessels out of Bristol were engaged in whaling, merchant service and coastal trade. A short wooden tower, built in 1846 was operated as a private aid but a more reliable beacon was needed to guide the traffic in the channel.

Congress approved funds for construction of a new lighthouse in 1854 and the structure was completed in 1855. The 28-foot brick tower was attached to the front of the keeper's house. A sixth-order Frensel lens, exhibiting a fixed white light, was installed in the wooden lantern room. In 1902 the light was electrified and upgraded to a fifth-order lens and in 1916 the wooden lantern room was replaced by an iron strucutre removed from the Roundout Lighthouse on the Hudson River.

The light was dismantled in1927; the replacement skeleton tower was subsequently discontinued upon completion of the bridge in 1930. In 1928 the property was sold to private ownership and, for a time, was rented to students from nearby Roger Williams University. After falling into disrepair, the property was purchased in 1991 and restoration completed; an automatic light, which comes on for two hours each night, was installed in the renovated lantern room. The property remains privately owned.

**Directions:** The lighthouse is located under the Mt. Hope River Bridge. From Bristol, follow Rt. 114 or 136 (which joins Rt 114) south. At the north end of the bridge turn east into Ferry Rd. and continue downhill to a parking lot. Park along Ferry Rd. or in the Roger Williams University visitors lot. The lighthouse can also be seen across the river from the south. (**Note map following page**)

# Hog Island Shoal Light

Dangerous shoals at the entrance to Bristol Harbor were initially marked by a small beacon boat placed at the southern end of Hog Island by a local steamship company in 1886. Because the dim light from this beacon failed to provide adequate guidance to mariners, a lightship from Fishers Island Sound was relocated to Hog Island Shoal in 1886. In 1896 Congress allocated funds for construction of a lighthouse to replace the lightship, by then in disrepair. Construction of the 60-foot cast-iron "sparkplug" style structure was completed in 1901.

A fifth-order Fresnel lens was originally installed, but replaced in 1903 with a fourth-order lens exhibiting a white flash. The caisson-supported tower has five decks, the first was the galley, the second and third were keeper's quarters. The light is now automated and has a modern optic. Views are possible from many points on shore and from the Mount Hope River Bridge. The light may be seen from the Bristol Ferry Light, however best views are from the water.

**Directions:** The lighthouse can be seen from the Mt. Hope Bridge or at a distance from a variety of shore locations near the Bristol Ferry Wharf. Best views are from the water via excursion boats from Warren, RI.

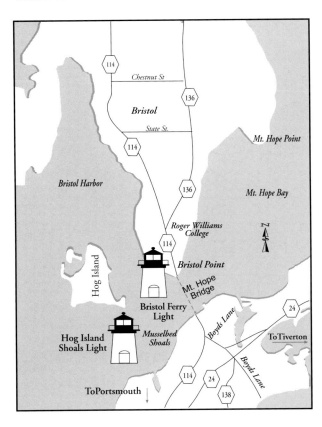

121

# Sakonnet Point Light

Rhode Island's easternmost light, located on the east side of the Sakonnet River, this lighthouse was initially planned for West Island. A group of influential cottage owners on the island protested this incursion into their retreat, so the lighthouse was sited on Little Cormorant Rock. Construction began in early1883, but harsh weather prolonged the completion until spring of 1884. The caisson-style cast-iron structure has three decks with living quarters on the first two and the lantern room on the third. A fourth-order Fresnel lens was installed, exhibiting a flashing white light.

The hurricane of 1938 caused a large crack in the base of the structure, with additional damage from another hurricane in 1954. Rather than fund the large repair costs, the Coast Guard discontinued the light in 1955. In 1961 the lighthouse was sold at auction and in 1985 donated to the Friends of Sakonnet Point Lighthouse. The group raised funds and undertook restoration and repair of the structure; additional funds from the Rhode Island Foundation were donated in 1994 and were used for further restoration.

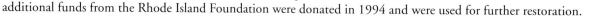

Sakonnet Point light was not relit until 1997; liability issues should the light fail caused the delay. With resolution of these concerns, the way was clear for the light to be operative again after 43 years. The light can be seen from the beach at Sakonnet Point in Little Compton but best views are by boat. **Friends of Sakonnet Point Lighthouse, PO Box 154, Little Compton, RI. 02837.**

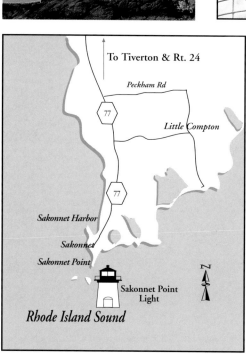

**Directions:** In Tiverton, follow Rt. 77 south to its end near the beach in the town of Sakonnet. Turn left into a narrow lane just before the beach parking area and continue to the end at a walled overlook. The lighthouse is offshore.

# Rose Island Light

Located in the east passage of Narragansett Bay just outside Newport Harbor, Rose Island was considered an important location for the defense of the Bay during the 18th century. Construction of Fort Hamilton was underway from 1798-1800, but the garrison was never completed or armed. Not until World Wars I and II were the structures used for storage of explosives used by the Navy's torpedo plant in Newport. In 1869 the present wood-framed lighthouse was built on the southwestern point of 17-acre Rose Island to guide mariners into Newport Harbor and assist in navigation of the east passage of Narragansett Bay. The design is similar to that of Pomham Rocks light and reflects a style known as French Second Empire Revival. The lantern was lit in January, 1870 with a sixth-order Fresnel lens exhibiting a fixed red light; a fog bell was added in 1885 and the brick oil house in 1912.

**Assistant Keeper "*Wiggins*" and his house**

123

# Rose Island Light

The lifestyle of the lightkeeper and family often involved challenges in terms of getting food and supplies to the lighthstation. One long-term keeper, Jesse Orton(1921-1936) kept a cow to supply milk for the family. The arrival of the animal apparently became much more of an event that planned. After purchase, the cow was loaded onto the Jamestown ferry; things initially went smoothly until the captain tried to guide the ferry through shallow water close enough to shore to drop a gangplank for offloading the animal. When it was clear this approach wasn't working, Elsie the Cow was lowered into the water. She paddled toward land, just barely making shore before she collapsed on the beach. Her ordeal behind her, Elsie recovered quickly none the worse for her adventure.

With construction of the Newport Bridge in 1969, Rose Island Light was no longer important for navigation and the station was decommissioned by the Coast Guard in 1971. Badly vandalized in the 1980s, the lighthouse was declared surplus. Although the property was initially offered to the City of Newport at no cost, a group of concerned citizens realized that upkeep and restoration of the lighthouse would present financial difficulty. The Rose Island Lighthouse Foundation was formed and took over the property in 1985.

Restoration to the 1912-1915 period was accomplished and in 1992 the Foundation opened the location to the public. On August 7, 1993 Rose Island Light was relighted as a private aid to navigation. As a "living museum", the lighthouse is available for overnite stays during season.

For information: **Rose Island Lighthouse Foundation, PO Box 1419, Newport, RI. 02840 (401) 847-4242. Website:** *www.roseislandlighthouse.org*

**Directions:** In season, the Newport and Jamestown ferry will stop at Rose Island on request and the Foundation also has a boat for access. Access is limited during part of the year to protect nesting birds. The lighthouse may be seen from the Jamestown-Newport Bridge and from excursion boats.

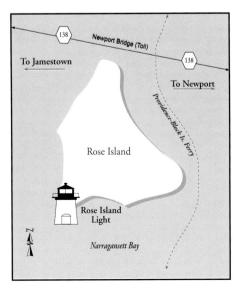

# Ida Lewis Rock (Lime Rock) Light

Built in 1854, the short stone tower with fixed red light originally was named after its location at Lime Rock, about 200 yards offshore. Initially there was no keeper's house so the keeper was required to row to and from the light, a distance now traversed by a boardwalk. A small keeper's dwelling was attached to the small tower in 1856. This lighthouse has become

famous not for its isolated location or impressive structure, but for the woman who is the most celebrated lighthouse keeper in American history, Idawalley Zoradia Lewis.

Ida's father, Hosea Lewis, a former coastal pilot from Hingham, Massachusetts, was the light's first keeper. His health became fragile in 1857, preventing him from continuing his duties and his wife was unable to take over, also due to frail health. Therefore, Ida, at age 16, took over the lightkeeping responsibilities in addition to caring for her four younger siblings.

Her daring rescues included four prominent young men whose boat had capsized, a schooner in distress, a drunken soldier, a number of sheep, and two soldiers from nearby Fort Adams. She was the first woman to receive a Congressional gold medal for heroism and became a legend in her own right, the focus of much attention and, to some extent, exploitation by others seeking to cash in on her name and fame. Along with a variety of publicity offers, Ida received countless unsolicited proposals of marriage. In 1870 she finally wed William Wilson of Connecticut who soon went missing and was not again seen. Despite her years of service and performance of the demanding keeper's duties, the tradition of the Lighthouse Service was followed which dicated she was not the "official" lightkeeper at Lime Rock. Her father remained, officially, in that position until his death whereupon her mother, again officially, succeeded him. Not until 1879, upon her mother's death, did the Lighthouse Service finally designate Ida Lewis as lightkeeper, with full recognition and status. Her lifesaving efforts continued throughout her tenure and she did not let age deter her efforts. At age 65 she completed her last rescue, pulling a friend who had fallen overboard from a small boat to safety. She is credited with as many as 25 rescues during her 55 years at the lighthouse.

*Image from Harper's Weekly*

In October of 1911, Ida Lewis fell ill from an apparent stroke which some suggest may have been brought on by reports that Lime Rock light was to be discontinued. She succumbed to her illness shortly afterward; she was 69. Flags throughout Newport were flown at half staff in her memory and vessels in the harbor tolled their bells in her honor. Congress, in 1924, voted to rename Lime Rock Light in memory of Ida Lewis and her distinguished service.

In 1927 the light was discontinued and replaced by a skeleton tower; that light was discontinued in 1963. The Ida Lewis Yacht Club now owns the buildings at the Lime Rock site with the light attached to the keeper's house now operated seasonally as a private aid and tribute to the lightkeeper. Because of the many additions to the buildings and close "quarters", the light is best viewed from the water. Lewis' grave is in the Common Ground Cemetery in Newport.

*Image from Harper's Weekly*

**Directions:** In Newport, follow Thames St. south to Wellington Ave. The lightstation is at the end of a boardwalk and is now quarters for the Ida Lewis Yacht Club. Best views are from the water.

127

# Newport Harbor (Goat Island) Light

The first lighthouse on Goat Island in Newport Harbor was a 20-foot stone tower completed in 1823. The light, put into operation in January, 1824 exhibited a fixed white light. Unfortunately the location of the lighthouse, on the southern tip of Goat Island, was not ideal and confused mariners. Many vessels went aground on the rocks at the northern tip of the island, prompting a decision to relocate the lighthouse to that northern point. The new 29-foot stone structure and breakwater were completed in 1842(the original tower was later moved to Prudence Island in 1851). A new keeper's dwelling was not built until 1864; a fourth-order Fresnel lens was installed in 1857 and a fog bell added in 1873.

128

The light was electrified in 1922. After a submarine rammed the pier in 1923, badly damaging the foundation of the keeper's house, the structure was removed and never rebuilt. In 1963 the light was automated and now exhibits a flashing green light. A path from the hotel rear parking lot leads around to the lighthouse. The American Lighthouse Foundation now manages and oversees upkeep of the structure. **American Lighthouse Foundation, PO Box 889, Wells, Maine 04090 (207) 646-0515.** Website: *www.lighthousefoundation.org*

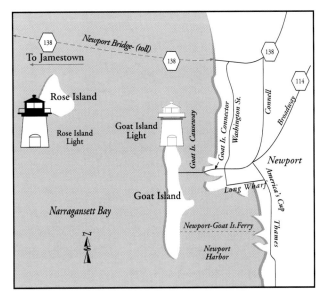

**Directions:** The lighthouse is on the grounds of a hotel and are easily accessible. **Coming into Newport via Rt. 138,** follow the signs to Historic Newport which take you in town via Connell Highway, to America's Cup Ave. Turn right (east) onto the Goat Island Connector (at the Visitors Center). Continue over the causeway to the motel parking lot and the lighthouse. **From Rt. 114 into Newport:** Follow Rt. 114 (Broadway) into the historic district--signs direct you. From America's Cup Ave., turn east at the Goat Island Connector, continue over the causeway to the motel parking lot and the lighthouse.

# Castle Hill Light

The property for the lighthouse at Castle Hill was not come by easily. Congress authorized funds in 1875 for a fog signal to guide mariners through the East Passage of Narragansett Bay. The site chosen for the signal was on the property where a prominent Harvard professor owned a summer cottage (now the Castle Hill Inn). He refused to sell, noting that he and others in the area thought noise from the signal would intrude on their peaceful setting. However, in 1886 a lighthouse was proposed for the site as well, further complicating the professor's life.

Finally, in 1887, the property owner relented; he sold a portion of his land to the government but would not grant access through his land for construction and steep cliffs precluded landing by boat. In 1888 right-of-way was granted and construction of the 25-foot granite lighthouse began in 1889; the keeper's house was at Castle Hill Cove. A fifth-order Fresnel lens was installed, exhibiting a flashing red light. The station also had a fog bell, which served to annoy the professor. Although the bell was discontinued after only 18 months, a few years later an even larger and louder bell was installed. The top half of the tower was painted white in 1889.

After the keeper's house was destroyed by a hurricane in 1938, the light was automated in 1957 and a modern optic replaced the Fresnel lens. All other outbuildings were removed. A path from the Castle Hill Cove Marina leads through the woods to the lighthouse.

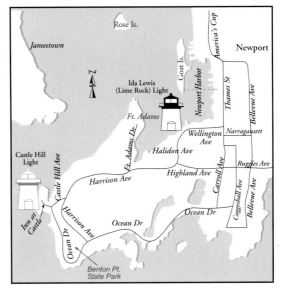

**Directions:** From Newport, follow America's Cup Ave. south to Thames St, then to Wellington Ave. Turn right (east) onto Wellington and continue to the intersection with Halidon Ave; turn south (left) onto Halidon. Bear right onto Harrison Ave., then right into Castle Hill Ave. Turn left onto Ocean Drive, then bear shortly right onto the Inn at Castle Hill Rd. and continue to the Castle Hill Inn grounds. There is a small sign and path to the lighthouse at the Inn. Parking is also available at the Castle Hill Cove Marina with a trail to the lighthouse that begins opposite the marina entrance.

131

# Warwick Neck Light

A 30-foot tower attached to the roof of a small stone keeper's house was the first lighthouse on Warwick Neck. Built in 1826, the light was intended to guide mariners between the neck and Patience Island. In 1831 a larger, wood-framed dwelling was added to the smaller building. A fourth-order Fresnel lens replaced the original system of lamps and reflectors in 1856.

A severe storm in September, 1869 caused extensive damage to the New England coast; a significant portion of the bank near the lighthouse was taken by the storm as well. In 1889 a new Victorian-style keeper's house was built to replace the smaller dwelling which was then used as a barn. In 1932 a new 51-foot steel tower was built.

Years of gradual erosion also took a toll and, by the 1930s, Warwick Light was threatened by the encroaching sea. Then, in 1938 a hurricane caused so much additional erosion that the new lighthouse was literally on the edge of the cliff. In 1939 the tower was relocated to its present site about 50 feet inland, remaining in service throughout the move. The light was automated in 1985 and a modern optic replaced the Fresnel lens. A Coast Guard family now lives in the keeper's house. Although the lighthouse can be seen through the gate at the station, best views are from the water.

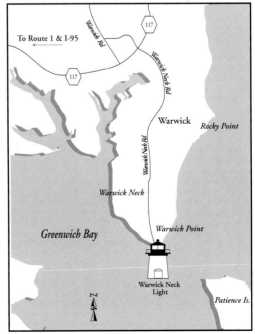

**Directions:** Whether coming from the north (Apponaug) or south (Shawomet), follow Rt. 117 (west Shore Rd) to the intersection with Warwick Neck Ave. Turn south and continue to the lightstation.

# Conanicut Point Light

Located on the north end of Conanicut Island, the lighthouse was built in 1886 to guide mariners navigating the dangerous area. The tower is attached to a square wood house; the two-story dwelling is notable for the gingerbread trim and simple frame construction which sets it appart from other Rhode Island lighthouses.

A fifth-order Fresnel lens was installed, exhibiting a fixed white light, later changed to fixed red in 1907. The light was discontinued in 1933 and the lantern room removed. The property was sold at auction and the replacement skeleton tower also discontinued in the early 1980s. Trees now obsure a good view of the structure.

**Directions:** From Jamestown follow Rt 138 to East Shore Rd and turn north. When East Shore Road turns to the west, turn instead to the **right** onto a dirt road. The lighthouse is on the left, about 0.1 mile from the turn. Trees largely block the view and the road is a narrow, private lane. (**Note map following page**).

*Photograph courtesy U.S. Coast Guard*

# Plum Beach Light

This 54-foot "coffee pot" lighthouse was built in 1896-99 to guide mariners through the West Passage of Narragansett Bay, the most direct route for shipping traffic headed to Providence. Construction at this location was particularly difficult due to rough waters. Plum Beach is one of 11 lighthouses built using the pneumatic caisson method in which a multi-sectioned caisson was assembled, taken to the site and lowered to the seabed. Water was then pumped out of the empty bottom section while the uppermost sections were filled with concrete, allowing the structure to sink 30 feet into bedrock. A fourth-order Fresnel lens was installed and the light put into service in 1899.

The foundation of the lighthouse, already cracked by ice during the winter of 1918, was further damaged by the Hurricane of 1938 but at least it remained standing; several lighthouses were destroyed or irreparably damaged.

Construction of the Jamestown Bridge in 1941 made the Plum Beach light unnecessary; it was discontinued and abandoned. Although the Coast Guard maintained the lighthouse became state property by right of eminent domain, the state refused to take ownership. In 1988 a Massachusetts development enterprise offered to purchase the structure for use as a lighthouse museum in Quincy, MA. Word of this intent spread and a group of local residents formed The Friends of Plum Beach Lighthouse in order to keep "their" light in place. The question of ownership continued to be a sticking point and the structure continued to deteriorate.

A 1998 Superior Court ruling finally allowed that the state owned the lighthouse, enabling the Friends group to pursue acquisition of the structure, accomplished in October, 1999. Although a $500,000 federal grant was earmarked for restoration and repair, the lighthouse is still in need of significant work at this time. **Friends of Plum Beach Lighthouse, Inc., P.O. Box 451, Portsmouth, RI. 02871.**

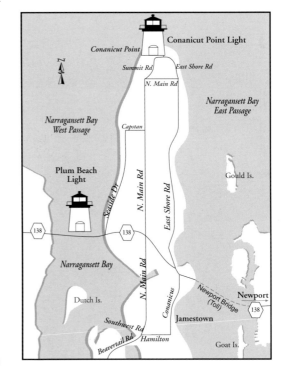

**Directions:** From Rt 138 turn north onto Seaside St. The lighthouse can be seen from points along the shore or from the Jamestown Bridge. If coming from Conanicut Point, follow N. Main St. south; turn west onto Capstan St. and continue to Seaside St. Turn south and follow Seaside; the lighthouse is offshore to the right. Excursion cruises from Warren pass this light.

# Poplar Point Light

Although it has the distinction of being Rhode Island's oldest, unrebuilt tower still standing on its original foundation, the Poplar Point lighthouse was only in use 49 years. Built in 1831, the octagonal wooden tower is attached to the roof of the one-story wood-framed keeper's house. The original Winslow Lewis system of eight lamps and reflectors, was replaced in 1855 with a fifth-order Fresnel lens, exhibiting a fixed white light.

The new Wickford Harbor light, 200 yards offshore from the Poplar Point Light, was put into service in 1880 and in 1882 the Poplar Point light was discontinued, then sold to private ownership. Only the topmost portion of the lantern is visible from Poplar Point Lane; a walk down to the beach and around behind the house gives better views. Views also are possible from the breakwater at Sauga Point, across Wickford Harbor.

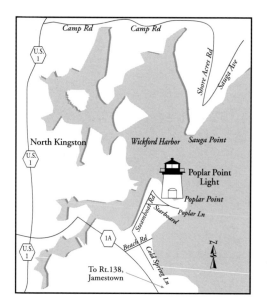

**Directions:** Only the topmost part of the lighthouse is visible from the front, at the end of Poplar Lane. Walking down to the beach and around behind the property gives better views. The Wickford Harbor Breakwater off Sauga Point also offers views. **To Poplar Lane:** Heading south on US Rt 1 from North Kingston or North from Route 1A from Jamestown via Rt 138, turn east onto Beach Rd.Continue to the intersection with Cold Spring Rd, turn left, then right onto Steamboat Rd. Follow that road to Poplar Lane. The area is private, but parking at the curb to walk the beach is permitted.
**To Wickford Harbor:** From US Route 1 (north or south) turn east onto Camp Ave. and continue to Shore Acres Rd. Follow that road to the intersection with Sauga Ave. Parking is permitted on both roads to this point. A pathway just to the right of the curve leads to the beach and the breakwater.

# Dutch Island Light

The first lighthouse on the island was built in 1826 to mark the west passage of Narragansett Bay and to guide vessels into Dutch Island Harbor. A trading post was established early on to barter with local Indians, exchanging Dutch goods for furs, meat and fish--thus giving the island its name, "Dutch Island".

Located at the southern tip of the island, the first lighthouse was attached to the keeper's house and contained a Winslow Lewis lighting system. Construction of the first 30-foot stone tower and keeper's house was shoddy at best. An inspection report by the Lighthouse Service from 1844, notes the dwelling to be the state's worst example of lighthouse construction. Repeated requests for upgrade were not acted upon until 1857 when funds were appropriated for rebuilding of the tower and renovation of the dwelling. The present 42-foot brick tower was attached to a new keeper's house and a fourth-order Fresnel lens installed, exhibiting a fixed white light. This characteristic was changed to occulting red in 1924 and automated in 1947.

*Photograph courtesy U.S. Coast Guard*

The property was declared surplus in the 1950s and returned to the state; the keeper's house collapsed shortly thereafter. Vandals extinguished the light in 1979 and it was then officially discontinued. The property was left to fall into ruin, although the island remains a part of the Bay Islands Park system, owned by the state of Rhode Island. Although the Coast Guard still owns the lighthouse, it was leased in 2000 to the American Lighthouse Foundation; this organization plans to work with local groups and residents toward restoration and renovation of the site. Views are possible from the Fort Getty Recreation Area but best viewing is by boat. **American Lighthouse Foundation, PO Box 889, Wells, ME 04090 (207) 646-0515** *www.lighthousefoundation.org*

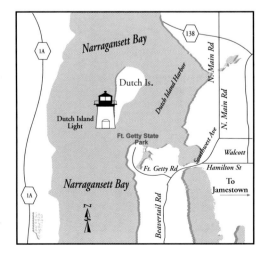

**Directions:** The light is best viewed by boat but may be seen from the Jamestown Fort Getty Recreation Area. Take Rt.138 and North Main Rd to Jamestown. Bear right onto Southwest Ave. and continue to the park entrance. Follow the perimeter road; views are possible from the high ground overlooking the bay.

# Beavertail Light

During the Revolutionary War, the British occupied Newport. Without access to Narragansett Bay, Rhode Island could not participate in the rebellion. The state then was slow to ratify the Constitution and to cede the lighthouse at Beavertail to the Federal Government in 1793; a stipulation was added that, if a proper state of repair and function was not maintained, the state would reclaim the light.

The original 58-foot wooden lighthouse at Beavertail was built in 1749, the third in the American colonies (after Boston Light and Brant Point on Nantucket). Funding was obtained by a tax on cargo entering the port of Newport. This structure apparently burned in 1753 and was rebuilt the

following year of brick and rubblestone. The lantern held a spider lamp with 15 whale-oil burning wicks and nine-inch reflectors. As a parting shot, the British burned the lighthouse as they withdrew in 1779, reportedly removing the lighting system as well. President Washington authorized repairs in 1790. In 1815 a hurricane destroyed the original keeper's house which had been located too near the water; a stone dwelling was built to replace it.

Beavertail light then was used as an experimental site for gas lighting. Coal was burned to generate the gas and it was piped to the lamps via design similar to that used for residential gas ceiling fixtures. Whale oil merchants were not pleased by the switch and successfully lobbied the Lighthouse Service to abandon the experiment. A variety of fog signal apparatus also was used at the station: a bell (1829), air whistle and air trumpet operated by compressed air (1851), steam whistle (1857), hot air engine powered signal (1868), compressed air siren (1900), diaphragm horns and finally the current electronic fog signal.

A new 45-foot square granite tower was built in 1856 and still stands. A third-order Fresnel lens was installed and a larger brick keeper's house also constructed. The light was electrified in 1931.

The Hurricane of 1938 took a severe toll at Beavertail; the keeper's daughter was killed when her school bus was overturned on the way to the lighthouse. His son, also onboard the bus, and the driver were the only survivors of the accident. Another hurricane in 1954 caused structural damage to the keeper's house but no lives were lost. The light was automated in 1972 and a modern optic replaced the Fresnel lens. Now located within Beavertail State Park, the station is easily accessible; the assistant keeper's house now houses the museum displaying the fourth-order Fresnel lens which replaced the original third-order optic. The Beavertail Lighthouse Museum Association oversees maintenance of the station. **Beavertail Lighthouse Museum Assoc., P.O. Box 83, Jamestown, RI. 02835.**

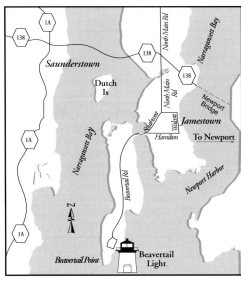

**Directions:** From Jamestown, head south on N. Main St. or Walcott Ave. (see directions for Dutch Island Light). At the intersection of Southwest Ave. and Hamilton Ave, turn onto Beavertail Rd. Follow the road to its end at a parking area for the light (Beavertail State Park).

# Point Judith Light

Point Judith is a mile-long finger of land extending from the coast, with the entrance to Narragansett Bay to the north and Block Island Sound to the south. Frequent fog and dangerous ledge to the west made navigating passage around the point treacherous and an early beacon was likely placed in the late 1700s. A variety of explanations can be found for the naming of the area, but one is particularly colorful. The story goes that a Nantucket sea captain found himself lost in the fog off the point. His daughter, Judith, shouted that she saw land but the captain could see nothing but thick fog and replied "P'int Judith, p'int".

The first lighthouse at Point Judith, the third in Rhode Island, was built in 1810. The octagonal wooden tower, with a system of spider lamps and 15 whale oil-burning wicks, only lasted five years before succumbing to a hurricane in September, 1915. The following year a 35-foot stone tower was built with a revolving light using a Winslow Lewis system of 10 oil-fueled lamps and reflectors. The light was made revolving to distinguish it from the Beavertail Light; one revolution of the weighty mechanism took more than two minutes.

In 1857 the present 51-foot, octagonal granite tower was built, connected to a brick keeper's house by covered walkway. A fourth-order Fresnel lens was installed, and a fog signal added in 1867. The tower originally was all white, the top half painted brown at a later time. In 1872 the signal was replaced by a fog whistle after complaints that the sound could not be distinguished from that of the surf. A brick oil house was added in 1917 and a new fog signal building in 1923.

New and larger quarters were built by the Coast Guard in 1937 and additional outbuildings added. The 1857 brick keeper's house was razed in 1954; an assistant keeper's house from 1874 also was subsequently destroyed. The oil house and fog signal building remain as does the original fourth-order Fresnel lens. The light was automated in 1954 and remained an active Coast Guard station until 1995. The grounds are open and easily accessible.

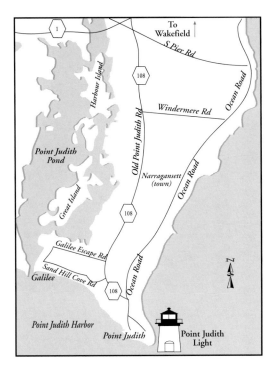

**Directions:** From US Route 1, turn south onto Rt.108 (Old Point Judith Rd). Continue to the end of this road; turn right onto Ocean Rd. and continue to the lighthouse and parking area.

141

Sandy Point extends several miles into Block Island sound; the area also is known for dangerous shoals and frequent fog. Block Island North light was intended to warn mariners away from the shoals and to mark the entrances to Block Island Sound and Long Island Sound.

There were initially two 45-foot wooden towers, built in 1829, on opposite sides of a wood framed keeper's house. The structure soon was threatened by erosion and, in 1837, a new lighthouse was built a short distance inland. Again two towers were attached to opposite ends of the granite dwelling. Howver, the lighting systems did not produce sufficiently intense beams and mariners complained that, from more than three miles, the two lights blended into one. Once again erosion claimed the structure, and construction of another structure still further inland was required in 1857; it too was taken by the elements.

Finally, in 1867 the present 52-foot granite lighthouse was built 700 yards from the point, surrounded by a 2-1/2 story dwelling. The style is similiar to that seen at Great Captain Island, Sheffield Island and Morgan Point lights in Connecticut. A fourth-order Fresnel lens was installed, exhibiting a fixed white light, later changed to flashing. The light was electrified in the 1940s.

# Block Island North Light

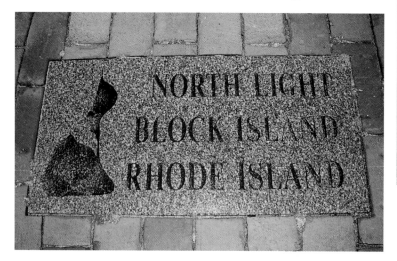

142

Block Island North light was automated in 1956 and deactivated in 1973. The U.S. Fish and Wildlife Service subsequently acquired the station and surrounding acreage as a refuge for many bird species. The lighthouse was left unattended and fell victim to vandalism; in 1984 it was sold, along with two acres of land, to the Town of New Shoram for $1.00. The town received a grant in 1989 for restoration of the lighthouse and successfully petitioned the Coast Guard to return the "official light" from the skeleton tower back to the North Light. The original Fresnel lens is on display in the restored first floor, now a museum. Plans are for continued restoration of the second and third floors and lantern room. To accomplish this, the North Light Commission sold bricks which are placed in an apron around the lighthouse. Long term plans include a live-in caretaker and conversion to wind power. **North Light Commission, c/o Town Hall, P.O. Drawer 220, Block Is., RI 02807.**

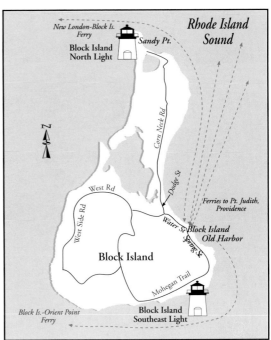

**Directions:** Ferries to the island depart from Galilee (near Pt. Judith, RI) New London (CT), and Providence, RI. **To the North Light:** From the ferry landing at Old Harbor, follow Water St. and Dodge St. to Corn Neck Rd. Turn right onto Corn Neck Rd ad continue to the road's end and a small parking area. Walk 0.5mile along the beach to the lighthouse.
**To the Southeast Light:** From the ferry landing at Old Harbor, follow Water St. to Spring St; continue on Southeast Light Rd to the lighthouse, located on Mohegan Bluffs.

143

# Block Island Southeast Light

Funds originally appropriated in 1856 for construction of a lighthouse at Mohegan Bluffs, on the southeastern tip of Block Island, were diverted to rebuild the Block Island North Light. Not until 1872, following petition by a local merchant, was funding authorized by President Grant for the Southeast light. The cost was staggering--$80,000 with $10,000 for the first-order Fresnel lens.

Established in February, 1875, the Southeast Light was designated a primary seacoast light, meaning it was equipped with the most powerful lighting apparatus available-- a first-order lens and lamp with four circular wicks which dropped through the tower to its base, coming to rest in a barrel of whale oil. One-half inch of the wicks was consumed daily and 900 gallons of oil annually. In 1880 a new first order lens system was installed which rotated on a mercury bath driven by a weight-powered clockwork mechansim which required rewinding every four hours.

The octagonal brick tower with 16-sided cast-iron lantern, is attached to the 2-1/2 story duplex keeper's house with identical 1-1/2 story wings in the back. A fog signal was installed in 1906; the present electronic fog signal was installed in 1974. In 1929 the characteristic of the light was changed to flashing green from fixed white in order to distinguish it from other area lights.

In 1990 the Coast Guard deactivated the Southeast Light. At that time it was clear the structure was endangered due to years of erosion; only 50 feet of land then separated the light from the sea (the building was originally 300 feet inland). The National Trust for Historic Preservation listed the Southeast Light as one of America's most endangered structures. To fund the approved relocation of the lighthouse away from the cliff, the Block Island Southeast Lighthouse Foundation raised approximately $2 million from private and Federal contributions. In August, 1993 the relocation began, including removal of the lens and mercury bath. A new first-order Fresnel lens, formerly in the Cape Lookout (NC) light, was installed and the light relit in August, 1994. The rock in lower righthand photograph marks the site of the lighthouse prior to being moved. Block Island Southeast Light was given National Historic Landmark designation in 1997; recent (2001-present) extensive repairs and restoration are ongoing. *(Note map and directions on page 143)*

**Block Island Southeast Lighthouse Fnd., Box 949, Block Island, RI. 02807 (401) 466-5009.**

# Watch Hill Light

History suggests that Watch Hill was so named because it was used as a lookout point by the Narragansett Indians and that a small beacon and watchtower were built on the site by the colonial government of Rhode Island in the mid 1700s. Because there is a dangerous reef southwest of the point, a lighthouse was proposed to mark the eastern entrance to Fishers Island Sound in 1793, but not until 1806 were funds for construction authorized by President Thomas Jefferson.

The first lighthouse at Watch Hill, Rhode Island's second built in 1809, was a 35-foot wooden tower with a system of whale oil lamps and parabolic reflectors. To distinguish it from the light at Stonington, CT., the Watch Hill beacon was changed to rotating in 1827. By 1855 the initial structure faced threat of erosion and a new tower was constructed about 50 feet northwest of the first. The 45-foot tall, 10-foot square granite tower was lined with brick and a fourth-order Fresnel lens installed, exhibiting a fixed white light. At this time a two-story brick keeper's house also was added and a granite sea wall built around the perimeter of the property. This station and that at Beavertail are similar in architectural design.

The Watch Hill light is distinguished by its roster of keepers, including Sally Ann Crandall who, in 1879, became the first woman to keep the light following her husband's death. She was then succeeded by Fanny K. Sckuyler in 1888.

This area has seen its share of maritime mishaps. In 1872 the steamer *Metis* collided with a schooner and began sinking near Watch Hill. Area residents helped rescue 33 passengers, but 130 lives were lost. Subsequently a U.S. Life Saving Service Station was located at Watch Hill. Then, in 1907, the steamer *Larchmont* collided with a schooner during a blizzard, resulting in the loss of 150 lives. The life saving station was abandoned in the 1940s and destroyed in 1963.

The light was automated in 1986 and a modern optic replaced the Fresnel lens. Buildings are now leased to the Watch Hill Lightkeepers Association which hired a resident keeper to maintain the station. The oil house now serves as a seasonal museum.

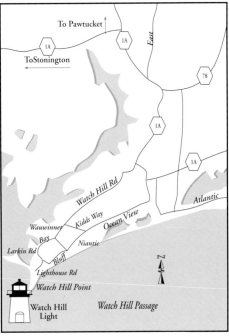

**Directions:** From Route 1A, turn south onto Watch Hill Rd. Bear right to Wauwinnet Rd, then left onto Bay St and left again onto Larkin Rd. Lighthouse Rd. is to the right, just before coming to Bluff Rd. Visitors must park outside Lighthouse road and walk to the station.

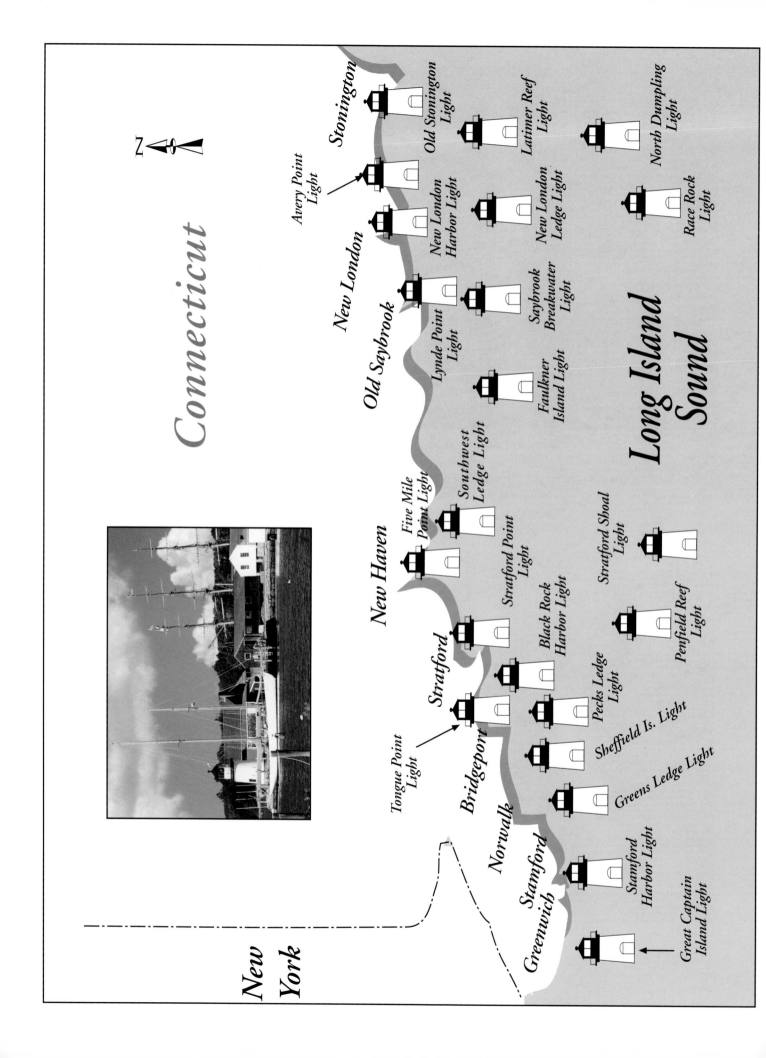

# The Connecticut Lighthouse Tradition

*Compiled by Ted Panayotoff*

The Connecticut coastline is, in large part, sheltered from the Atlantic Ocean by Long Island and as such became an important commercial maritime highway as early as Colonial times. Lighthouses aided navigation to these safe harbors as Long Island Sound became important for coastal and oceanic trade.

The history of Connecticut lighthouses begins in October 1760 when the General Assembly of the Colony of Connecticut, responding to a petition from New London merchants, authorized construction of a lighthouse on the west bank of the Thames River at New London. The 64 ft. tower of dressed stone was financed by lottery and funds appropriated by the Assembly. Lit 1761, this light was the fourth of 12 lighthouses built in the American Colonies between 1716 and 1788. Following its establishment in 1789, the U.S. Lighthouse Service assumed responsibility for all U.S. lighthouses making Connecticut's New London Harbor Light a U.S. lighthouse in 1790.

The U.S. Lighthouse Service sought to further development of coastal and international maritime trade by constructing lighthouses to mark prominent harbors, significant landfalls and dangerous shoal areas. In Connecticut this program began in 1801 with two tapered octagonal lighthouse towers of brownstone—an 80 ft. tower at New London Harbor which replaced the 1761 tower and, in 1802, a similar 40 ft. brownstone lighthouse on Faulkner Island to mark a dangerous reef. Less expensive wooden towers were built at Lynde Point at Saybrook (1803), at Five Mile Point in New Haven Harbor (1805) and on Fayerweather Island at Bridgeport Harbor (1809). These economical structures proved short lived and all three soon were replaced with the brownstone tapered octagonal style. All five still stand. Another wooden lighthouse at Stratford Point, built in 1822, fared better but was replaced by a cast iron tower in 1881.

Stone lighthouses generally were superior to wooden structures, but still suffered the effects of erosion. Built in 1824, the original Stonington Harbor Lighthouse, the easternmost lighthouse on the Connecticut mainland, had to be rebuilt in 1840 further inland. In 1889 this lighthouse was replaced by the cast iron Stonington Breakwater Light while the old lighthouse was used as the keeper's dwelling until 1910. Other stone lighthouse towers built in Connecticut in the early 1800's were at Sheffield Island (1828), Great Captain Island (1829) and Morgan Point (1831). In 1868 these stone towers were replaced by similar and distinctive granite Victorian style structures with the lighthouse tower integral with the two story keeper's dwelling.

In the next decade the Lighthouse Service addressed the challenge of marking several significant off shore reefs, ledges and shoals. This endeavor required construction on small wave-swept rock outcroppings. Granite structures were built at Penfield Reef (1874), Stratford Shoal (1877) and Race Rock (1879). All were similar, with granite dwelling and integral granite towers. The New Haven Southwest Ledge Light (1877), also a caisson light on an offshore ledge, initiated cast iron as a construction material for Connecticut lighthouses. The cast iron Second Empire style two story superstructure and light tower is unique to Connecticut lights. This design may have been chosen because the New Haven light was to be featured at the U. S. Lighthouse Service exhibit at the 1876 Centennial Exposition in Philadelphia. Unfortunately, another identical structure was exhibited.

After the brief experiment with cast iron, a simpler, more utilitarian and cost effective design was adopted. These lighthouses, all built between 1882 and 1906 and often called "spark plugs", are prevalent along the New England and Middle Atlantic coasts. Five of this style structure are still standing in Connecticut. The last lighthouse built in Connecticut was New London Ledge Light (1909) at the entrance to New London Harbor. This unique structure has a granite and concrete caisson foundation with a three story superstructure of brick and concrete. The distinct architectural style, a combination of Colonial Revival and French Second Empire styles, is often used to symbolize all Connecticut lighthouses.

# Old Stonington Harbor Light

Windmill Point, on the west side of the harbor, was the site for the first lighthouse at Stonington. The 30-foot stone tower and keeper's house were built in 1823; a Lewis system of 10 lamps and reflectors was installed, exhibiting a fixed white light. Only sixteen years later the sea had claimed all but 30 feet of the bluff and the lighthouse itself was in danger. The government decided that relocation of the structure to the east side of the harbor was the best solution.

In 1840 a new lighthouse, built largely from the disassembled original structure, was completed. The octagonal granite tower was raised to 33 feet and the stone keeper's house attached. Another Lewis lighting system was installed which was replaced in 1865 with a sixth-order Fresnel lens. Construction of a 25-foot cast-iron breakwater light in 1889 made the initial lighthouse obsolete and it was sold to private ownership in 1908. The breakwater light was subsequently replaced by a skeleton tower in 1926.

In 1925 the Stonington Historical Society acquired the lighthouse and converted it into a museum, displaying the sixth-order Fresnel lens and other exhibits of local history and the lighthouses of Long Island Sound. **Stonington Historical Society, PO Box 103, Stonington, CT. 06378.**

**Directions:** From Mystic, CT or Westerly, RI areas, follow Route 1, then 1A to Stonington. Turn south onto Water St. and continue to the town center and to the road's end at a parking area/beach just beyond the lighthouse (signs to the Lighthouse Museum direct you).

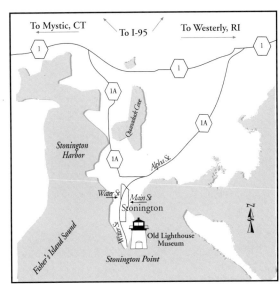

# Latimer Reef Light

Treacherous Latimer Reef at the east end of Fisher's Island Sound, four miles southeast of Mystic, Connecticut, is marked by this lighthouse. A typical offshore cast-iron "sparkplug" style structure, the 49-foot tower was built in 1884 with three stories of living space, a watch deck and lantern room. The original fifth-order Frensel lens was upgraded to fourth-order in 1899.

In 1974 the light was automated; the Fresnel lens was removed in 1983 and replaced by a modern optic. Best views are by private boat although distantly visible from the parking area at the Old Stonington Lighthouse. (*Lighthouse noted in red on map*)

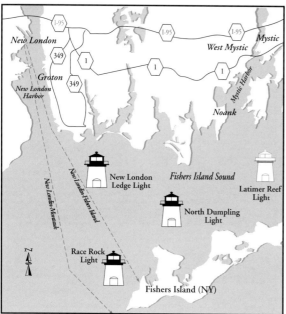

# North Dumpling Light

Located in Fisher's Sound, this station was first established in 1847. The present structure, similar to others in the area, including Penfield Reef to the south, was built and the beacon lit in 1871. The 31-foot octagonal brick tower originally held a fifth order Fresnel lens; a modern optic is now installed. Following automation in 1959, the light was moved to a nearby steel skeleton tower and the North Dumpling property sold to private ownership.

Vandalism took a heavy toll however, as the new owner was infrequently at the site. In 1980 the property was again sold; the new owner remodeled the keeper's house, successfully petitioned to have the optic returned to the lantern room and the skeleton tower removed. By 1987 the island was again for sale, this time purchased by an interesting individual who attracted brief fame to himself and his island after an unsuccessful encounter with bureaucratic red tape. Apparently the

owner was initially denied permission to build a windmill to power his generator and countered by declaring himself Lord of Dumpling II, reigning over the sovering nation appropriately named the North Dumpling Republic. National media of varying outlets picked up the story; at one point the owner noted that his plans were to open the lighthouse to the public. That proposal, and his other "adventures" have faded with time.

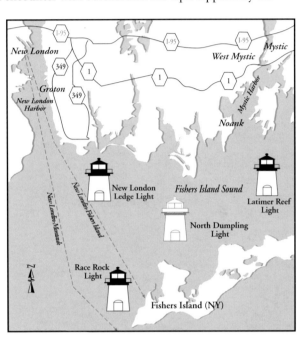

The original dwelling has been greatly augmented and altered, along with the addition of numerous other structures. The lighthouse must be viewed by boat.

**Directions**: The lighthouse is visible distantly from ferries to Fisher's Island(NY) and Orient Point(NY) from New London,CT. (*Location indicated in red on map.*)

# Race Rock Light

Located off the western end of Fisher's Island, the light marks a dangerous reef which, in the early 1800s, claimed ships at an alarming rate. The structure, built in 1879, was considered a benchmark in lighthouse engineering. It is a caisson structure built on ledges which had to be enlarged. Strong currents made this a daunting task which was finally accomplished by dumping thousands of tons of multi-ton granite boulders around the reef to create an artificial island. The entire construction project took almost eight years to complete.

The 45-foot granite tower is attached to the side of a 1-1/2 story keeper's house similar in design to that of Stratford Shoal. A fourth-order Fresnel lens was originally installed. In 1978 the light was automated and a modern optic placed. The lighthouse must be viewed by boat.

# Avery Point Light

The 55-foot tower on the University of Connecticut Avery Point Campus was built in the early 1940s as a memorial to the Coast Guard's lightkeeping tradition. Although not officially established, the light was maintained as a private aid to navigation, initially displaying a flashing white characteristic which was later changed to flashing green. In 1944 Avery Point was acquired for use as a Coast Guard Training Center. The symbolic, low-powered private aid was discontinued when the Center closed in 1967 and the lighthouse became the property of the state.

In 1997, the deteriorating condition of the tower prompted officials at the University to declare it a safety hazzard. An effort was initiated to restore the structure, with cost estimates in the range of $75,000. That figure has now risen well into the $100,000-plus range. The American Lighthouse Foundation in 1999 began fundraising for the restoration; contributions are still sought. **American Lighthouse Foundation--Avery Point Fund--PO Box 889, Wells, ME.  04090.**

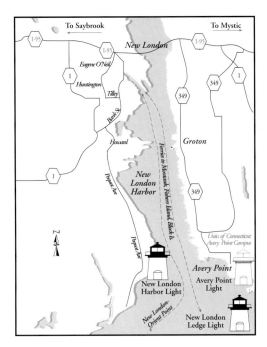

**Directions**: From I-95 take the exit to Route 349 south. Follow signs to Avery Point Campus, turning onto Rainville Ave. At Benham Rd., turn south (signs again direct you). Bear left into Eastern Point Rd and continue to its end at the campus. Drive into the campus and turn right at West St. and a parking area. The lighthouse is a short walk around to the tower.

# New London Ledge Light

In the early 1900s, the city of New London became an increasingly busy port as new industry replaced whaling and the existing harbor light was not adequate to guide mariners around the dangerous ledge at the harbor entrance. A lighthouse offshore, at the eastern end of Long Island Sound near the entrance to New London Harbor, was petitioned as early as 1890, but constrution did not commence until 1906 and the work not completed until 1909. The light originally was called Southwest Ledge Light, but soon renamed New London Ledge Light to avoid confusion with the light in New Haven Harbor, also a "Southwest Ledge Light". One of the last lighthouses built in New England, the brick and granite structure is unusual for an offshore location; it's said local residents wanted the building to blend in with their stately shorefront homes and create a pleasing visual presentation.

The cast-iron lantern originally held a fourth-order Fresnel lens, exhibiting three white flashes, followed by a red flash at 30-second intervals. In 1911 a fog signal was added to replace the one discontinued at the harbor light. A modern optic was installed in 1984.

Duty at this lighthouse at once offered solitude prized by many but also isolation which could drive others to madness; close quarters often resulted in heated "verbal exchanges". The wafting scent of summer barbeques coupled with the sight of young ladies at the beach (binoculars were kept at hand), made duty at a "more social" shore location all the more appealing. And there was the spirit of Ernie to contend with.

Legend tells that the infamous ghost, Ernie, is the spirit of a keeper who, in 1936, learned his wife had run off with the captain of the Block Island Ferry. Unable to handle this news, the keeper proceeded to throw himself from the roof of the lighthouse into the sea--or perhaps he simply fell to his death. In any event, since then unexplained happenings have been attributed to "Ernie's" spectre--doors open and close themselves, televisions turn on and off, decks are mysteriously swabbed, the fog horn and light behave erratically and securely tied boats are set adrift. One disgruntled keeper noted that the entire lighthouse was "Ernie's domain".

This location was the last manned lighthouse in Long Island Sound. Following automation in 1987, solar panels were installed. A group of local citizens soon formed the New London Ledge Lighthouse Foundation to preserve the lighthouse, establish an educational center and open the light to the public. Renovations and repairs were undertaken in 1994 and arrangements were made to establish boat transportation to the location. Work and fundraising are ongoing, with future intent to offer overnite accommodations at the lighthouse or "Ernie's Place".

**New London Ledge Lighthouse Foundation, PO Box 855, New London, CT 06320.**

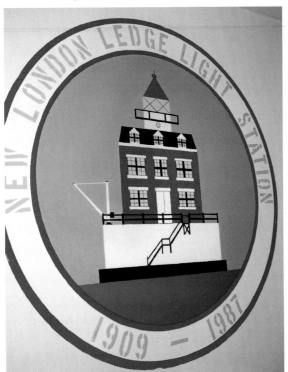

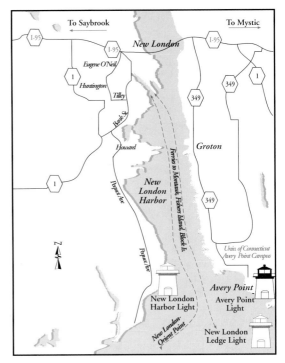

**Directions:** The lighthouse can be seen from several points on shore in New London and Groton area. Trips to the light are available in season through Project Oceanology at the Avery Point Campus of the University of Connecticut. See directions for Avery Point Light. Signs on campus guide you to the Project buildings.

# New London Harbor Light

Trailing only New Bedford and Nantucket, New London was America's third leading whaling port in the mid 1800s. Although in the early 1700s some sort of beacon marked the harbor and a dangerous nearby ledge, the first permanent structure, a 64-foot stone tower with wooden lantern, wasn't built until 1760. The New London lighthouse was the fourth in North America and the first on Long Island Sound. Funds for construction were raised by selling lottery tickets and a port tax contributed to upkeep of the tower.

By 1800 there was a 10-foot crack in the tower wall and other repairs were needed. Mariners also found that the tower did not stand out adequately from nearby homes. A new 89-foot ocragonal tower was built in 1801, along with a keeper's dwelling and oil house. It is the oldest existing lighthouse in Connecticut. The present 2-1/2 story keeper's house was built in 1863. In 1857 a fourth-order Fresnel lens replaced the original Argand-style system of lamps and reflectors. A series of fog signals was tried at the New London station, all of which thoroughly frayed the nerves of local residents and prompted one gentleman to quip that the area would soon be noted for the prevalence of nervous disorders. Eventually a "quieter" fog trumpet was installed and eventually the signal relocated to New London Ledge Light.

The light was automated in 1912 and the property sold at auction. Although visible from the road, best views are from an excursion boat or ferry from New London.

**Directions**: From I-95, take the exit for Rt. 84 south into New London. Follow Eugene ONeill Pkwy south, bear right onto Huntington St. Turn left at Tilley St., then right onto Bank St. Take another left at Howard St., then bear right into Pequot Ave, following that road around a rotary, south to the lighthouse. The area is congested; keeping the harbor to your left, continue south to the residential area. The tower is on private, well-posted property; visitors are not welcomed. (*Map preceding page*).

# Saybrook Breakwater Light

A large sand bar at the entrance to the harbor at Old Saybrook is marked by this light, built in 1882 at the end of the newly constructed breakwater. Located 1-1/2 miles from the Lynde Point beacon, the Saybrook Breakwater light was put into service in 1886 and became known as the Outer Light. The 49-foot cast-iron tower was originally fitted with a fifth-order Fresnel lens, exhibiting a fixed white light with red sector; in 1890 a fourth-order lens was installed. The original 1889 fog bell was extemely large and the noise upset local residents, prompting installation of a much smaller bell which was later removed and replaced by a fog horn.

The Hurricane of 1938 destroyed the bridge to the breakwater and the platform around the lighthouse, but the tower survived. In 1959 the light was automated, the Fresnel lens removed and a modern optic installed. The road to the breakwater is private and shore viewpoints are distant; best views are by boat. Some Connecticut automobile license plates feature this lighthouse.

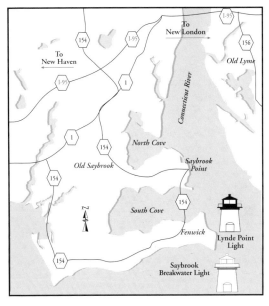

# Lynde Point (Old Saybrook Inner Harbor) Light

The original 35-foot wooden tower was built in 1802 to mark the entrance to the Connecticut River and Old Saybrook Harbor. Mariners thought the light too dim and too short, but rather than simply raise the tower, a new 65-foot granite lighthouse was built in 1838. The original lighting system of ten lamps and reflectors was replaced by a fourth-order Fresnel lens in 1852, then in 1890 with a fifth-order Fresnel optic exhibiting a fixed white light. A fog bell was added in 1854. The small 1833 wooden keeper's house was replaced in 1858 by a larger dwelling attached to the tower. Despite protests by the Saybrook Historical Society, in 1966 the Coast Guard razed that structure and built the present utilitarian duplex.

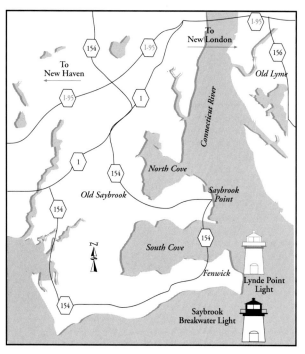

The Saybrook BreakwaterLight was put into service in 1886 and became known as the Outer Light; the Lynde Point light was thereafter referred to as the Inner Light. Although the light was automated in 1978, the fifth-order Fresnel lens remains. Coast Guard personnel live in the duplex. The road to the light runs through an exclusive community and is not typically open to the public; shore views are distant.

**Directions:** From I-95, take the exit into Old Saybrook via US 1/ CT 154. Signs direct you when approaching from either direction. In Old Saybrook center, turn left and follow Rt 154 to Saybrook Point marina and dock. Access to the lighthouse is via private, residential area and may be difficult.

Although the campus of Yale College is New Haven's most well known presence, Five Mile Point also boasts a storied past dating to the American Revolution. Well before a lighthouse was located at the site, a fierce battle was joined when British troops attempted to land there and march into New Haven. American rifleman repelled that effort and two casualties of that encounter are buried near the present lighthouse.

Following the war, trade flourished in the port of New Haven. The initial lighthouse, a 30-foot octagonal wooden tower, was built on the east side of the harbor entrance in 1805. Five Mile Point refers to the distance from downtown New Haven. In 1835 a 2-1/2 story keeper's house was added. The visiblity of the light was eventually deemed inadequate and the tower itself thought to be too low. In 1847 a new 65-foot sandstone tower was built, attached to the keeper's dwelling. A fourth-order Fresnel lens replaced the original system of twelve lamps and reflectors. In the 1860s a fog bell was added.

# Five Mile Point
# (New Haven Harbor) Light

With construction of a light at Southwest Ledge in 1877, the Five Mile Point beacon was no longer needed and therefore discontinued. The city of New Haven acquired the property in 1922; a number of years later, in 1949, Lighthouse Point Park was opened. Major renovations were accomplished in 1986. The 82-acre park is open year 'round; the lighthouse is depicted in one of the panels on the antique carousel in the park.

**Directions:** From I-95 take Exit 50N or 51S to Townsend Ave. Following signs to Lighthouse Park, turn right (south) onto Townsend Ave., and continue to Ligthouse Rd. Turn right and follow the road to the park entrance. An antique carousel is located near the lighthouse.

*The carousel*

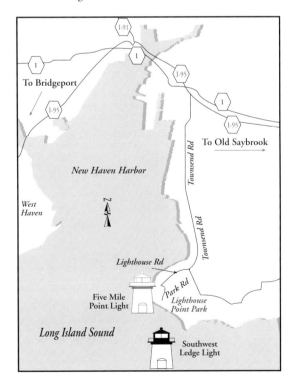

165

# Faulkner's Island Light

This 40-foot octagonal stone tower was built in 1802 to warn mariners from the rocks surrounding the three-acre island in Long Island Sound, about three and one-half miles offshore from Guilford, Connecticut. The state's second oldest lighthouse is also the only active light on an island in the state. A Winslow Lewis system of 12 whale-oil lamps and reflectors was the original lighting system, replaced in 1840 with an improved Lewis system. A fourth-order Fresnel lens was installed in 1856; an outside spiral stairway was added in 1871 since the larger Fresnel lens did not allow for trap door access to the lantern from watchroom below. The original keeper's house was rebuilt in 1858.

The island was often a busy place, hosting large groups of summer day visitors. One keeper raised twelve children on the island while another practiced his hobby of taxidermy on the unfortunate birds who crashed into the lighthouse and his musically inclined family played impromtu recitals for island visitors. In 1976 the 1871 keeper's house was destroyed and in 1978 the light was automated, the Fresnel lens replaced by a modern optic. The light was solarized in 1988.

Erosion has been a constant threat to the light on Faulkner's Island. Over the years, the sea has encroached on the structure at a rate of at least six inches per year so that only about 35 feet of bluff separate the tower from the water. Following years of neglect and vandalism, a local resident founded the nonprofit Faulkner's Light Brigade in 1991 to raise funds for relocation and restoration of the lighthouse. In 1999 a significant restoration of the tower to the 1871 period was completed. Erosion measures undertaken in the fall of 2000 by the Army Corps of Engineers included restoration of vegetation to the bluff and construction of a 1,350 foot stone revetment along the island's east side. Comparable measures have been successful at Montauk Point light on Long Island.

Part of the Stewart B. McKinney National Wildlife Refuge, the island is now a stop on the migratory path for more than 150 species of birds and hosts one of the largest breeding colonies of roseate terns in the northeast. The light must be viewed by boat.

Fund raising for continued restoration work and erosion measures is ongoing. **Faulkner's Light Brigade, PO Box 199, Guilford, CT   06438.**

*Photo courtesy U.S. Coast Guard*

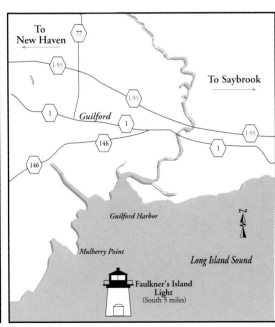

# Southwest Ledge Light

Although in 1845 a lighthouse was proposed for this treacherous ledge, approximately one mile offshore on the east side of the entrance to New Haven Harbor, the isolated location made the project cost prohibitive at that time. Engineering technology also was not up to the task. By 1873 construction at Southwest Ledge had become feasible and the resulting structure was one of the first built on a cylindrical iron foundation, designed to prevent floating ice from becoming trapped. A major winter storm that year required suspension of the work until spring of 1874.

The superstructure for the lighthouse had been completed ahead of schedule and was displayed at the Centennial Exposition in Philadelphia until 1876. Ironically, that structure was then sent to Delaware and an identical 45-foot cast-iron tower placed at Southwest Ledge. The light was put into service in January, 1877; the light at Five Mile Point was extinguished that same day. A fourth-order Fresnel lens was installed, exhibiting a fixed white light; a red sector was added in 1889 to warn mariners of Branford Reef and Gangway Rock.

Life at this station was isolated and apparently caused one keeper's nerves to fray entirely. Reportedly assistant keeper Nils Nelson, a large man in stature, despaired of the living conditions and, without apparent provocation, began chasing the keeper with a fire ax in hand. The assistant subsequently departed the premises in a rowboat after his superior took refuge in a storage area. No reports of the incident were made, as the more diminutive keeper feared reprisal; instead he brought is brother-in-law to the lighthouse for protection. This move did not deter the assistant who again went berserk, this time wielding a butcher knife. The brother-in-law was able to subdue the assistant who again rowed to shore. Shortly thereafter Nelson took his own life in 1908.

Keepers were removed and Southwest Ledge light automated in 1953. A modern optic replaced the original Fresnel in 1988. The fog signal remains. Views are distant from shore locations or sightseeing cruises; best views are by private boat.

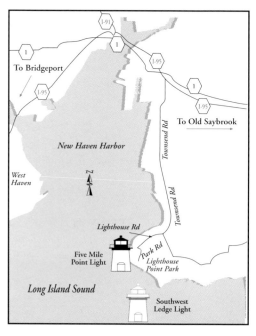

168

# Stratford Shoal Light

A lightship was originally stationed at Stratford Shoal, a dangerous three-quarter-mile long ledge in Long Island Sound, midway between Long Island and the Connecticut shore. Because the ship swayed heavily in bad weather and had difficulty staying at anchor, in 1873 the Lighthouse Board decided to built a lighthouse at the locations. Construction of the masonry structure took the better part of two years (1874-1876) to complete, due in part to weather delays.

The 35-foot granite lighthouse, attached to a 28-foot square dwelling, was put in service in December, 1877 with a fourth-order Fresnel lens showing a fixed white light. A fog trumpet was added in 1880. The location was particularly isolated and unforgiving, perhaps giving rise to the suicide attempt by one keeper. In 1905 the keeper went into a rage, locked himself into the lantern room and threatened to destroy the light. He emerged only to attempt to take his own life, but one of the assistants fortunately intervened; the keeper was subsequently released from the Lighthouse Service.

The original Fresnel lighting system was updated in 1894 and again in 1905; a modern aerobeacon was installed when the light was automated and keepers removed in 1970. The light is now solar powered. The light must be viewed by boat; the Bridgeport-Port Jefferson ferry offers distant views. (*Note map location in red*)

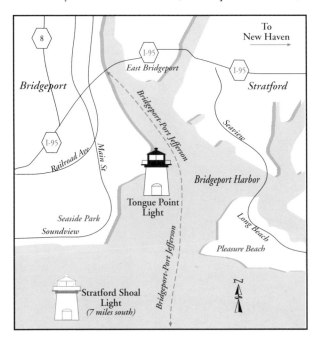

## Stratford Point Light

On the west side of the entrance to the Houstatonic River, this lighthouse was the third built by the government on Long Island Sound. The 28-foot octagonal wood tower and small keeper's house were built in 1822. An Argand system of ten lamps and reflectors was initially installed, then replaced by a fifth-order Fresnel lens in 1855. In 1864 a fog bell tower was added.

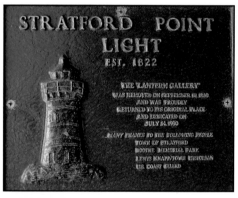

A new 35-foot cast-iron tower was built in 1881, one of the earliest of this design. At that time a new fog bell was added and a third-order Fresnel lens was installed, showing a flashing white light. In 1906 that lens was replaced by a fourth-order Fresnel optic which revolved in a bed of mercury.

A young girl also figured prominently in the history of this station. In 1871 the keeper's granddaughter, Lottie, was visiting when her father and grandfather had to aid a vessel in distress, leaving the twelve-year-old girl alone at the lighthouse. She noticed the light had gone out, climbed to the lantern room and lit a backup safety lamp. The captain of a passing steamer was able to discern the faint light and pass the area safely.

This lighthouse was "beheaded" in 1969, when the lantern was removed for installation of an automated aerobeacon. On display until 1990 in Booth Memorial Park in Stratford, the lantern was refurbished and returned to the tower that year when a smaller optic was installed. A Coast Guard family now lives at the station.

**Directions:** From I-95, take exit 30 to CT 113 (if southbound, turn south (left) onto Surf Dr. and continue to intersection with CT 113). Follow CT 113 toward Lordship and the airport. Turn left at Oak Bluff Ave (which is 113), continue around the rotary to Prospect Dr. Follow that road to its end at the lighthouse. There is a parking area, but the grounds are private.

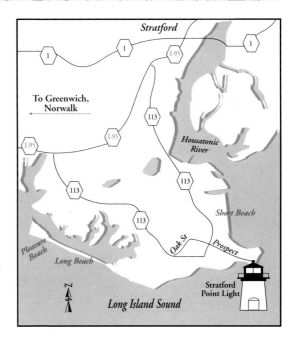

171

# Black Rock Harbor (Fayerweather Island) Light

Now connected to the mainland by breakwater, Fayerweather Island was years ago much larger and used for grazing sheep.

The first lighthouse, a 40-foot octagonal wooden tower, was built in 1808 on the south end of the island to mark the entrance to Black Rock Harbor. In 1821 a hurricane destroyed the initial structure; a 41-foot rubble stone tower was completed in 1823 to replace it. The first lighthing apparatus was a whale-oil spider lamp, replaced by a fifth-order Fresnel lens in 1854. The original keeper's house was replaced in 1879.

Stephen Moore, third keeper at Fayerweather Light, taught his daughter, Catherine, how to trim the wicks and care for the light when she was just 12 years old. As a young woman, when in 1819 her father was injured and disabled in an accident, Catherine assumed the full duties of lighthkeeper, although her father was technically the keeper until his death in 1871. He was 100 and she was 76; she continued at the station until age 83, resigning in 1878 to live on the mainland in a cottage overlooking Fayerweather Island. She lived to be 105.

The City of Bridgeport acquired the lighthouse after it was discontinued in 1933. Part of a recreation area established in part by P.T. Barnum, the structure fell victim to vandalism but remained structurally sound. Fire destroyed the keeper's house in 1977. In 1983 a local group, Friends of Seaside Park, and the Black Rock Community Council began a restoration and preservation effort; debris was cleared and the island established as a nature preserve with walking and hiking trails. Soon after, however, neglect and vandalism again took a toll. In 1993, as a result of particular concern for the lighthouse by two local residents, a lighthouse fund was established and an annual fund raising event was initiated.

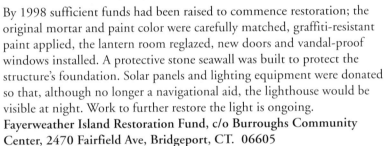

By 1998 sufficient funds had been raised to commence restoration; the original mortar and paint color were carefully matched, graffiti-resistant paint applied, the lantern room reglazed, new doors and vandal-proof windows installed. A protective stone seawall was built to protect the structure's foundation. Solar panels and lighting equipment were donated so that, although no longer a navigational aid, the lighthouse would be visible at night. Work to further restore the light is ongoing. **Fayerweather Island Restoration Fund, c/o Burroughs Community Center, 2470 Fairfield Ave, Bridgeport, CT. 06605**

**Directions**: From I-95, take the Worden St. exit and turn north onto Worden. Continue to State St. and turn right (east); follow State St. to Iranistan Ave. Turn south (right) onto Iranistan and continue to Seaside Park. Turn right onto Sound View Dr, then onto P.T. Barnum Blvd. to the parking area. The path to the lighthouse across the breakwater begins at the beach area .

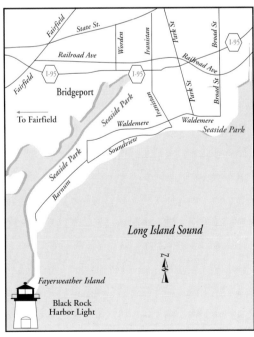

173

# Penfield Reef Light

Two hundred years ago this area was lush pasture land, supporting sheep and dairy cattle, but over the years the land was worn down, becoming a series of islands, then a sandbar, and finally a reef. One of the mostdangerous areas in Long Island Sound, this mile-long reef just south of Fairfield, CT., still plagues mariners even though marked by the light. There is often confusion of the Penfield Reef light with that at Stratford Shoal, midway between Long Island and Connecticut. Safe passage is not possible on each side of both lights and this critical difference has occasioned a significant number of shipwrecks in the area. The reef was unaffectionately labeled the "Blue Line Graveyard" when in 1916 a string of barges from the Blue Line Company went aground there.

After the Civil War, Bridgeport prospered and the harbor became a bustling center for trade. Constrution began on the 35-foot octagonal tower and attached two-story stone house in 187. The station was one of the last offshore masonry structures completed before the cast-iron caisson style became standard. In 1874 the light was put into service, with a fourth-order Fresnel, exhibiting a flashing red light. A fog bell was initially installed at the station, later replaced by a fog horn, then in 1892 by a fog trumpet.

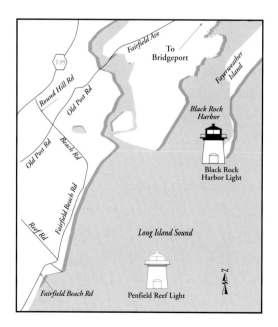

In December, 1916, when heading for the mainland to join his family for the Christmas holiday, the keeper's dory overturned in rough seas. Despite rescue attempts, the assistant keeper could not save him. Legend tells that months later a ghostly presence was seen gliding down the tower stairs. Upon checking the station's log, the keeper noted it was open to the December 22, 1916 entry, the night of the failed rescue. Tales of unexplained happenings continued for years following the tragedy: mariners still report the spectre of a lightkeeper on the lantern room or hovering around the reef, a mysterious figure in a rowboat reportedly guided a boater to safety then vanished, another shadowy figure plucked two boys from the water as they struggled to right their capsized boat, only to vanish soonafter. A significant number of rescues also were performed by "real" keepers at Penfield Reef, but one episode offered particular compensation for their efforts. Twenty seven passengers were taken from the treacherous waters after their pleasure boat that went aground on the reef; one passenger offered the keepers one dollar, which was refused.

The light was automated in 1971 but local residents objected to plans for a pipe tower replacement. Federal and state Congressional representatives were enlisted in efforts to save the lighthouse. A modern optic was installed and the Fresnel lens removed. The structure has not been cared for and is slowly falling into ruin. Distant views are possible from Fairfield Beach; it's also possible to walk part way to the light at low tide. Best views are by boat.

# Tongue Point (Bridgeport Breakwater) Light

Located at the end of a breakwater, about 500 yards offshore, the black 21-foot cast-iron lighthouse was built in 1895 to mark the east end of Tongue Point on the west shore of Bridgeport Harbor. A sixth-order Fresnel lens was installed, exhibiting a fixed white light. No keeper's quarters were built. The keeper at Bridgeport Harbor Light also initially tended the Tongue Point Light but soon took it upon himself to hire an assistant to take over the harbor light duties. This unauthorized action could have resulted in his termination from the Lighthouse Service, but he lucked out and was allowed to retain his position at Tongue Point and another keeper hired for the harbor light duty.

When the shipping channel was widened, the breakwater was shortened and the lighthouse moved 275 feet toward shore. The light was automated in 1954 and the Fresnel lens was replaced by a modern optic in 1988; the characteristic is now flashing green. Plans by the Coast Guard to remove the light altogether in 1967 were not well received by local boaters and the plans were abandoned. The lighthouse is located on the property of a power station; it may be seen from Sound View Park or from aboard the Bridgeport-Port Jefferson ferry.

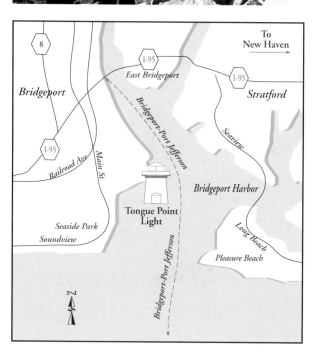

**Directions:** The Bridgeport-Port Jefferson ferry passes close by the light; from I-95 take the Water St. exit and follow signs to the Long Island ferry. Distant views are possible from across the harbor; take Exit 29 from I-95 to Seaview St. Follow Seaview south to Central St. The lighthouse is visible at the road's end at the bridge.

# Pecks Ledge Light

Built in 1906 to mark Pecks Ledge at the east end of the Norwalk Islands in Long Island Sound, this 54- foot lighthouse is another of the cast-iron "sparkplug" style. A fourth-order Fresnel lens was initially installed, showing a flashing white light. The tower has three levels for living space, topped by the watchroom and lantern.

The light was automated in 1933 and in 1939 the Fresnel lens was removed. A much weaker lens was installed at that time, then in 1989, an even less powerful lens was mounted atop the tower's roof. Both vandalism and nesting birds have taken a toll on the structure. Although visible distantly from Calf Pasture Beach and the Sheffield Island ferry, best views are by private boat.

**Directions:** From I-95, Take the exit to East street and continue to the intersection with VanZant St (CT 136). Turn east onto Cemetery Blvd and then south onto Gregory Blvd. Continue south on Gregory to the intersection with Fifth St. & Calf Pasture Beach Rd. Bear right onto Calf Pasture Beach Rd and continue to the beach. The lighthouse is visible distantly off shore.

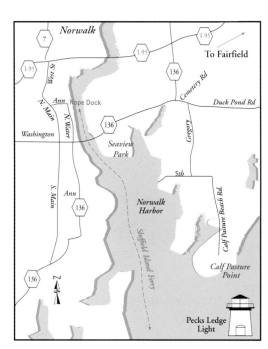

# Sheffield Island Light

Captain Robert Sheffield purchased White Island in 1804 and it was thereafter known as Sheffield Island. The the first lighthouse on the 53-acre island, a wooden tower built in 1826, was maintained by Captain Sheffield's son-in-law, whose residence/keeper's house was a small 1-1/2 story granite structure which still stands on the northeast side of the present lighthouse. A system of lamps and parabolic reflectors turned by clockwork mechanism was initially used, replaced in 1857 with a fourth-order Fresnel lens.

The present stone lighthouse was built in 1868, similar in style to those seen at Great Captain Island and Block Island North Lights. In 1902, with completion of Greens Ledge Light, Sheffield Island Light was discontinued and sold at auction two years later. Over the years a variety of unfortunate enterprises, including a resort and commune, came and went on the island; fires, vandalism and neglect took a severe toll. In 1986 the Norwalk Seaport Association acquired the lighthouse, keeper's house, stone cottage and surrounding four acres. The U.S. Fish and Wildlife Service manages the remaining 59 acres as the Stewart B. McKinney National Wildlife Refuge.

The Association began fund raising for restoration of the lighthouse and property and in 1993 major work was completed, including addition of electricity to the keeper's house. A severe storm that fall undid much of the restoration work, but a year later the lighthouse had been again repaired and was opened to the public. In 1997 measures were taken to slow erosion near the lighthouse and in 1998, mounting expenses required to maintain the lighthouse resulted in a major deficit in funds. Another fund raising campaign was mounted and a loan secured to pay off the mortgage on the lighthouse, but major debt is still outstanding. The Association offers tours of the lighthouse in season; there is ferry service from the Hope Dock in Norwalk. **Norwalk Seaport Association, 132 Water St., South Norwalk, CT. 06854. (203) 838-9444.**

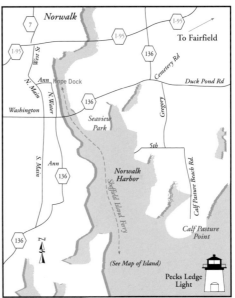

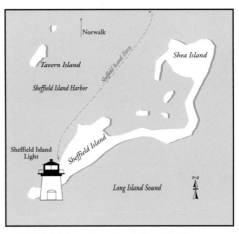

**Directions:** From I-95 North, take Exit 14N to South Norwalk/Maritime Aquarium. Fairfield Ave., then Reed St. will take you onto West Ave. Continue on West St. bearing left onto North Main St. Turn left at Ann St. and continue to Water St. Turn right onto Water St.; the Hope Dock and ferry are about 1/4mile on the left with limited parking. From I-95 South, take Exit 15S (CT7, Danbury, Maritime Aquarium. Turn left onto West Ave., and follow the above route. Regardless of direction of approach to Norwalk, following the signs to the Maritime Aquarium will take you to the Hope Dock area.

# Greens Ledge Light

The 52- foot cast-iron, sparkplug-style lighthouse was built on a ledge west of Sheffield Island light in 1902 to guide mariners through the west entrance to Norwalk Harbor. A fifth-order Fresnel lens was originally installed, showing a flashing red light. That lens was replaced only a few months later by a fourth-order lens exhibiting a white light with red flashes. Over the years Greens Ledge Light developed a slight structural tilt, which was exacerbated by pounding sustained in the Hurricane of 1938. This situation was not sufficiently grave for concern, although vibrations would cause furnishings to slide to one side.

The lighthouse was automated in 1972 and the Fresnel lens removed. Efforts by the Coast Guard to interest a nonprofit group in assuming responsibility for care of the lighthouse have not been successful. Distant views are possible from some shore locations in Norwalk, but best views are by boat.

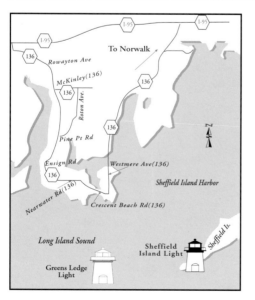

**Directions:** The light may be seen distantly from the ferry to Sheffiled Island and from Crescent Beach in Norwalk. From I-95 north, take Exit 12 then turn south onto Rowayton Ave (C T136). Turn left at McKinley St,then right at Roton Ave.. Bear left into Pine Point Rd, then continue around onto Pine Point Terrace, Gull Rd, then Ensign Rd (taking you through a residential area toward the water). Turn left onto Cresent Beach Rd then onto South Beach Dr. The light is offshore. Following CT 136 south from Norwalk onto Bluff Drive will also take you to South BeachDr.

# Stamford Harbor Light

For a number of years mariners had petitioned for a lighthouse on Chatham Rock, a rocky outcropping on the southwest end of Harbor Ledge on the west side of Stamford Harbor, before funds were appropriated for the construction in 1881. Sections of the cast-iron tower were assembled on a cylindrical 28-foot pier; the tower has five decks and is a typical "sparkplug" style structure. A fourth-order Fresnel lens was installed and the light put into service in 1882.

This lighthouse has two particularly grim tales associated with it. The first unfortunate episode occurred in 1927 when a keeper's daughter refused to leave the lighthouse to live on shore with her husband. Apparently he finally convinced her to accompany him to shore one day but, once ashore, promptly shot her, then himself. The second incident involves a keeper who, in 1931, was missing for three days before it was noted the lighthouse was not being lit. His body was found floating closeby and his boat recovered. Cuts on his head have led some to suggest he'd been pushed from the lighthouse, although it is probably more likely his boat simply overturned.

The Coast Guard discontinued the light in Stamford Harbor in 1953; a weaker light was subsequently installed and the lighthouse used as a private aid to navigation. From 1955 through 1982 the property was passed among a variety of private owners, one of whom did significant repair and restoration to the lighthouse. However, in 1996 the property again was offered for sale but remains unsold as of 2002. Although visible from several points on shore in Stamford, best views are by boat.

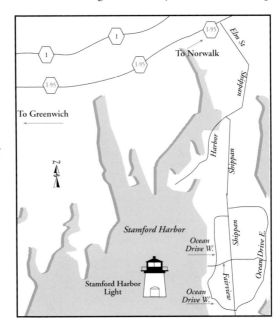

**Directions:** From I-95 north take Exit 8 to Magee, then Elm St. Continue to the intersection with Shippan, bear left onto Shippan and continue to Ocean Dr. Turn right onto Ocean Dr., then right at Fairview Ave and continue to the dead end. The lighthouse is visible distantly offshore from the beach.

# Great Captain Island Light

Land was purchased for construction of a lighthouse on the southeast tip of the island without knowledge that a site at Stamford Point also was still under consideration. The slight confusion was resolved without problem and, in 1829, the original 30-foot stone lighthouse was built along with a five-room keeper's house and system of lamps and reflectors. A fourth-order Fresnel lens was installed in 1858, exhibiting a fixed white light.

Earlier reports of shoddy construction and disrepair proved accurate and, by 1867, a new tower was needed. A new granite keeper's house with cast-iron tower attached to the front of the roof was completed in 1868; the Fresnel lens was reinstalled. A fog whistle was added in 1890 and upgraded to a siren in 1905. Local residents were soon taken aback by the sudden increase in noise produced by the new apparatus, prompting subsequent modulation of the signal to an acceptable level.

During prohibition bootleggers used the island as a handy, yet well-hidden, spot to dilute smuggled foreign liquor. The watered-down product was then taken to the mainland for sale. A series of clubs and casinos also have been located on the island.

The light at Great Captain Island was replaced by a skeleton tower in 1970 and the structure was immediately subject to vandalism. In 1973 the Town of Greenwich acquired the lighthouse and surrounding property; the town had previously acquired most of the island in 1966. Resident caretakers prevented further vandalism and in 1998 the Greenwich Chamber of Commerce began efforts to relight the beacon and renovate the structure. That work is ongoing. The ferry to the island is open to Greenwich residents only.

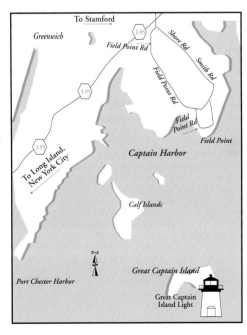

183

# Lighthouse Cruises and Tours

Visitor centers typically offer brochures and schedules for lighthouse tours in a particular area, with current information and ferry schedules. The following is only a partial list of available excursion options; new trips are added each season and others may be discontinued or modified.

## Massachusetts

<u>Cape Ann</u>-- most tours originate from Gloucester waterfront.

**Ten Pound Island Shuttle**--from Gloucester. The seasonal water taxi makes 'round trips to the island, the Gloucester waterfront and Rocky Neck art colony.

**Cape Ann Lighthouse Cruise**-- Harbor Tours departing from the Harbor Loop area. (978) 283-1979. The whale watching trips pass Ten Pound Island and Eastern Point as do "amphibious" sightseeing tours from Gloucester.

**Thacher Island**--The Thacher Island Association runs periodic cruises which take in all the light-houses in the Cape Ann area. (978) 546-7697

<u>The Boston Harbor Islands, North and South Shore</u>-- The islands are now a National Park Recreation Area so there are a variety of excursions out of Boston which will pass lighthouses of the inner islands, including access to Boston Light on Little Brewster Island.

**Friends of Boston Harbor Islands**--seasonal trips to the island, cruises which pass a number of lights on the north and south shore(s). Call for specific information: (781) 740-4290 Web site: *www.fbhi.org* .

**Boston Harbor Explorers**-- trips and schedules vary seasonally (617) 479-1871

**Friends of Flying Santa**--offers periodic trips to view the lights of Boston Harbor, north and south shores (617) 925-0783

**Island Alliance**--trips to Boston Light only (617) 223-8666

**Minots Ledge Light**--most of the above groups try to include Minots Ledge Light in at least one trip per season, but sea conditions are extremely variable and often preclude close viewing or force alteration in route.

<u>Cape Cod, Martha's Vineyard and Nantucket</u>--there are many harbor tours, ferries and whale watches which will pass some of the lights, but often distantly.

**Ferries**--to Martha's Vineyard from Woods Hole will pass Nobska, West Chop or East Chop lights. The ferry to Nantucket from Hyannis will pass South Hyannis and Pt. Gammon lights distantly and will pass Brant Point light on arrival in Nantucket. The "On Time" ferry from Edgartown to Chappaquidick offers a view of Edgartown Harbor light from the water. The Provincetown-Boston and Provincetown-Gloucester ferries pass Race Point, Long Point and Wood End lights and others distantly en route destination.

**Long Point**--boat shuttle in season (800) 750-0898

**Cape Cod Museum of Natural History**--offers day and overnight trips to Monomoy Island during the season. (508) 896- 3867. Website: *www.ccmnh.org*. The Audubon Society also offers trips from Wellfleet. The location is remote and rustic and sea conditions often require schedule changes.

**Nantucket and The Vineyard**-- a variety of tours available on both islands include the lighthouses. Four wheel drive vehicles are required to access Cape Poge Light on Chappaquidick and Great Point Light on Nantucket. Rentals are available on both islands.

# Rhode Island

## Block Island Lights

Ferries to the island are available from Galilee (RI) and New London (CT). Reservations for vehicles are required. (401) 783-4613 Website: *www.blockislandferry.com*. Email: interstate@blockislandferry.com.

## Rose Island Light

Stays are offered at the lighthouse during season. Visitors serve as "keepers". Transportation to the island is provided. Arrangements may be made by contacting the Rose Island Lighthouse Foundation, PO Box 1419, Newport RI. 02840 (401) 847-4242. The Foundation offers scheduled public tours during season. Contact them for specific schedule. Website: *www.roseislandlighthouse.org*.

The seasonal Newport-Jamestown ferry will stop at Rose Island on request for day visitors. Website: *www.jamestownri.com*

## Prudence Island Light  Ferry from Bristol to Homestead (401) 253-9808

## Bay and Harbor Cruises

Several lights may be viewed from cruises of Narragansett Bay (Rose Island, Hog Island Shoal, Bristol Ferry, Prudence Island, Newport Harbor, Ida Lewis, Castle Hill, Beavertail, Dutch Island, Plum Beach, Conanicut Point, Warwick Neck, Nayatt Point, Conimicut). The routes are variable and many views may be distant.

Bay Queen Cruises Warren, RI. 800-439-1350. Website: *www.bayqueen.com*

Any of the harbor cruises from Newport, RI will pass Rose Island, Castle Hill, Ida Lewis lights. The visitors center in Newport offers current schedule information.

# Connecticut

## Sheffield Island Light

The Norwalk Seaport Association sponsors a ferry to the island during season, leaving from Hope Dock in Norwalk. (203) 852-6241  Website: *www.seaport.org*

## New London Ledge Light

Trips to the lighthouse, passing Avery Point Light en route, are sponsored by Project Oceanology and the New London Lighthouse Foundation. Departures are from the Project Oceanology dock on the Avery Point Campus, University of Connecticut. (860) 445-9007, (800) 364-8472. Website: *www.oceanology.org*.

## Ferries, Cruises

The Bridgeport-Port Jefferson ferry passes close by Tongue Point Light. Stratford Shoal light is visible distantly en route. (203) 335-2040  Website: *www.bpjferry.com*

Ferries from New London to Fisher's Island,NY and Orient Point, NY will pass New London Ledge Light, New London Harbor Light, North Dumpling and Race Rock Lights (both distantly).

Harbor cruises fromMystic, CT. pass Morgan Point light.

Cap't John's Sport Fishing Center, Waterford, CT. offers a lighthouse cruise which passes the New London Harbor, Latimer Reef, Lynde Point, Saybrook Breakwater, and Race Rock lights (860) 443-7259 Website: *www.sunbeamfleet.com*

| LIGHTHOUSE | COLOR | CHARACTERISTIC | DESCRIPTION |
|---|---|---|---|
| **MASSACHUSETTS** | | | |
| Newburyport Range Lights (Inactive) | NA | NA | NA |
| Newburyport Harbor (Plum Is.) | Green | Group occulting flashing 15 sec. | Height above water: 50ft Range: 10nm |
| Annisquam Harbor | White with red sector | Flashing 7.5 sec.with red sector | Height above water: 45 ft Range:White= 14, Red=11nm |
| Straitsmouth Island | Green | Flashing every 6 seconds | Height above water: 46 ft Range: 6 nm |
| Thachers Island | White | Flashing, five times at 20-second intervals | Height above water: 124 ft Range: 19nm |
| Eastern Point | White | Flashing 5 seconds | Height above water: 57 ft Range:24 nm |
| Ten Pound Island | Red | Equal interval, 6 sec. | Height above water:57 ft Range:5 nm |
| Baker's Island | White, red | Flashing, alternating white & red, each 20 seconds | Height above water: 111 ft Range:White=16, Red=13nm |
| Hospital Point Front Range | White | Fixed | Height above water: 70ft |
| Hospital Point Rear Range | White | Fixed | Height above water: 183 ft |
| Fort Pickering | White | Flashing 4 seconds | Height above water: 28 ft |
| Derby Wharf | | Flashing red 6 seconds | Height above water:25 ft Range: 4nm |
| Marblehead | White | Fixed | Height above water: 130 ft Range:7nm |
| Long Island Head | White | Flashing 2.5 seconds | Height above water:120ft Range: 6nm |
| Deer Island | Red, white | Alternating red/white flashing 10 seconds with red sector | Height above water:53ft Range: White=14, Red=10nm |
| The Graves | White | Flashing, twice each 12 sec. | Height above water:98 f t Range: 24nm |
| Boston Light | White | Flashing 10 seconds | Height above water: 102 ft Range: 27nm |
| Minots Ledge | White | Group flashing, 1-4-3 each 45 seconds | Height above water: 85ft Range: 10nm |
| Scituate | White | Flashing 15 seconds | Height above water: 70ft |
| Plymouth (Gurnet) | White, red sector | Group flashing alternate single & double white every 20 sec.includes red sector | Height above water:102 ft Range:White=16, Red=14nm |
| Duxbury Pier | Red | Group flashing 3 times each 10 sec. | Height above water: 35ft Range: 6nm |
| Cleveland Ledge | White | Flashing 10 seconds | Height above water: 74 ft Range: 17nm |
| Butler Flats | White | Flashing 4 seconds | Height above water: 53ft Range:4nm |
| Palmer Island | White | Flashing 4 seconds | Height above water: 42 ft Range:5nm |
| Ned Point | White | Flashing 6 seconds each 6 seconds | Height above water: 41 ft Range:12nm |
| Borden Flats | White | Flashing 2.5 seconds | Height above water: 47 ft Range: 11nm |
| Bird Island | White | Flashing 6 seconds | |
| Tarpaulin Cove | White | Flashing 6 seconds | Height above water:78ft Range:9nm |
| Wings Neck (Inactive) | NA | NA | NA |
| Sandy Neck (Inactive) | NA | NA | NA |
| Nobska Point | White with red sector | Flashing each 6 sec. | Height above water: 87ft,Range:White=16nm, Red=12nm |
| Bass River (West Dennis) | White | Flashing 6 seconds | Height above water: 44ft |
| Point Gammon (Inactive) | NA | NA | NA |
| Stage Harbor (Inactive) | NA | NA | NA |
| Monomoy Point (Inactive) | NA | NA | NA |
| Chatham | White | Group flashing white twice 10 sec. | Height above water: 80 ft Range: 24nm |
| Nauset Beach | Red, White | Alternate red & white lights flashing each 5 seconds | Height above water: 114 Ft, Range: White=23, Red=19nm |
| Highland (Cape Cod) | White | Flashing 5 seconds | Height above water: 183 ft, Range: 23nm |
| Race Point | White | Flashing 10 seconds | Height above water: 45 ft, Range 16nm |
| Wood End | Red | Flashing 10 seconds | Height above water:45 ft, Range: 13nm |
| Long Point | Green | Flashing | Height above water: 36ft, Range: 8nm |
| West Chop | White | Occulting 4 seconds with red sector | Height above water: 84 ft Range: White=15, Red= 11nm |
| East Chop | Green | Equal interval each 6 seconds | Height above water: 79ft Range: 9nm |
| Gay Head | White, red | Flashing white alternating with flashing red each 40 seconds | Height above water: 170ft Range: White=24, Red=20nm |
| Edgartown Harbor | Red | Flashing 6 seconds | Height above water:45 ft Range: 5nm |
| Cape Poge | White | Flashing 6 seconds | Height above water: 65 ft Range:9nm |
| Brant Point | Red | Occulting 4 seconds, lighted 3 sec. | Height above water: 26ft, Range: 10nm |
| Sankaty Head | White | Flashing 7.5 seconds | Height above water: 158 ft Range: 24nm |
| Great Point (Nantucket) | White | Flashing white 5 sec. with red sector | Height above water: 71 ft Range:White=14, Red=12nm |

| LIGHTHOUSE | COLOR | CHARACTERISTIC | DESCRIPTION |
|---|---|---|---|
| **RHODE ISLAND** | | | |
| Beavertail | White | Flashing every 6 seconds | Height above water:64 ft  Range: 15nm |
| Block Island North | White | Flashing every 5 seconds | Height above water: 58ft  Range:13nm |
| Block Island Southeast | Green | Flashing every 5 seconds | Height above water: 261 ft Range: 20nm |
| Bristol Ferry (Inactive) | NA | NA | NA |
| Castle Hill | Red | Equal interval red 6 seconds | Height above water: 40 ft  Range: 12 nm |
| Conanicut Point (Inactive) | NA | NA | NA |
| Conimicut | White | Flashing 2.5seconds with red sector | Height above water: 58 ft  Range:White=15, Red=13nm |
| Dutch Island (Inactive) | NA | NA | NA |
| Hog Island Shoal | White | Equal interval 6 seconds | Height above water: 54 ft  Range:12 nm |
| Ida Lewis Rock | NA | NA | Private aid |
| Nayatt Point (Inactive) | NA | NA | NA |
| Newport Harbor | Green | Fixed | Height above water: 33ft  Range: 11nm |
| Plum Beach(Inactive) | NA | NA | NA |
| Point Judith | White | Group occulting 15 seconds | Height above water: 65 ft  Range: 16nm |
| Poplar Point (Inactive) | NA | NA | NA |
| Pomham Rocks (Inactive) | NA | NA | NA |
| Prudence Island | Green | Flashing 6 seconds | Height above water:28ft Range: 6nm |
| Rose Island | White | Flashing 6 seconds | Height above water:48ft |
| Sakonnet Point | Red | Flashing every 6 seconds | Height above water: 66ft |
| Warwick | Green | Occulting 4 seconds | Height above water:66 ft Range: 12nm |
| Watch Hill | Red, white | Alternating 5 seconds | Height above water: 61 ft ,Range:White=16, Red=14nm |
| **CONNECTICUT** | | | |
| Avery Point (Inactive) | NA | NA | NA |
| Black Rock Harbor(Inactive) | NA | NA | NA |
| Faulkner's Island | White | Flashing 10 seconds | Height above water: 94 ft, Range:13nm |
| Great Captain Island(Inactive) | NA | NA | NA |
| Greens Ledge | White, red | Alternating 24 seconds | Height above water:62ft  Range: White=17, Red=14nm |
| Lynde Point (Old Saybrook Inner Harbor) | White | Fixed | Height above water: 71 ft ,Range:14nm |
| Morgan Point (Inactive) | NA | NA | NA |
| New London Ledge | White, red | Group flashing 30 seconds | Height above water: 58ft, Range: White=17, Red=14nm |
| New London Harbor | White with red sector | Equal interval white 6 seconds, red sector | Height above water: 89ft, Range: White=17, REd=14nm |
| New Haven Harbor (Five Mile Point)-Inactive | NA | NA | NA |
| North Dumpling | White with red sector | Fixed, red sector | Height above water: 94ft, Range: 7nm |
| Pecks Ledge | White | Flashing 4 seconds | Height above water: 61ft, Range: 7nm |
| Penfield Reef | Red | Flashing 6 seconds | Height above water: 51ft, Range: 18nm |
| Race Rock | Red | Flashing 10 seconds | Height above water:67ft, Range:19nm |
| Saybrook Breakwater | Green | Flashing 6 seconds | Height above water: 58ft, Range: 11nm |
| Sheffield Island (Inactive) | NA | NA | NA |
| Southwest Ledge | Red | Flashing 5 seconds | Height above water: 57 ft, Range: 13nm |
| Stamford Harbor | White | Flashing 4 seconds | Height above water: 80ft, private aid |
| Stratford Point | White | Group flashing 20 seconds | Height above water: 52ft, Range: 16nm |
| Stratford Shoal (Middle Ground) | White | Flashing 5 seconds | Height above water: 60ft, Range: 13nm |
| Old Stonington Harbor (Inactive) | NA | NA | NA |
| Tongue Point | Green | Flashing 4 seconds | Height above water:31ft, Range: 5nm |

# Index

# Index

CatNap Publications